# Christian Hermit in an Islamic World

## A Muslim's View
## of Charles de Foucauld

by
Ali Merad

*Translated from the French with a
Foreword and Afterword by Zoe Hersov*

PAULIST PRESS
New York / Mahwah, N.J.

*Cover design by Nick Markell*

Originally published as *Charles de Foucauld au regard de l'Islam* by Editions Chalet in 1975. English translation copyright © 1999 by Paulist Press, Inc.

Library of Congress Cataloging-in-Publication Data

Merad, Ali.
    [Charles de Foucauld au regard de l'Islam. English]
    Christian hermit in an Islamic world: a Muslim's view of Charles de Foucauld / by Ali Merad ; translated from the French with a foreword and afterword by Zoe Hersov.
       p.  cm
    Includes bibliographical references.
    ISBN 0-8091-3903-0 (alk. paper)
    1. Foucauld, Charles de, 1858–1916. 2. Christianity and other religions—Islam. 3. Islam—Relations—Christianity. I. Title.
BX4705.F65M4713 1999
271'.79—dc21
                                        99-047039
                                           CIP

Published by Paulist Press
997 Macarthur Boulevard
Mahwah, New Jersey 07430

www.paulistpress.com

Printed and bound in the
United States of America

# Contents

# Translator's Foreword

IN 1975 THERE APPEARED IN FRANCE a small volume entitled *Charles de Foucauld au regard de l'Islam*,[1] written
by Ali Merad, a professor or Arabic literature and civilization at the University of Lyon. In it Merad considers
the "saint of colonialism" in his historical context, as a
Frenchman living at the end of the nineteenth and the beginning of the twentieth century. At the same time, and this is
his principal object, the author offers us the personal testimony of an Algerian Muslim as he contemplates the life of
the Christian hermit of the Sahara.

The book is, unfortunately, inaccessible. It is out of print
in French and has not been translated into English. The
problem is that the author assumes a knowledge of Charles
de Foucauld who, although a cult figure in France and in
some Catholic circles, is little known in the English-speaking
world.

Merad's work has a much wider potential audience that
should include all those with an interest in the relations
between Islam and the West, one of the great issues of our
time. For Islam can no longer be regarded as a religion of
backward peoples who live a comfortable distance away. The
Muslim world embraces countries in Africa, the Middle
East, the Indian subcontinent and Southeast Asia that are of
vital political and economic importance to the western

1

world. There are, too, substantial Muslim populations living in our midst, with their own distinctive concerns and a new political voice.[2] We are compelled to reckon with Islam as a reality that impinges on our lives.

Since Merad wrote optimistically of a peaceful Islamic renaissance, there have been great changes in the Muslim world. It is rare today to pick up a newspaper and not find some reference to Islamic extremists. The context is invariably one of violence associated with a "fundamentalism" that is equated with fanaticism. Recent events have rekindled the historic fear of Islam. Deep-rooted feelings of enmity and mistrust have been intensified and the gulf between us threatens to become unbridgeable.

At the same time there is growing disillusion with the Christian-Muslim that seems to have reached a dead end. On both sides there are those who find the whole enterprise too painful, too difficult and too hopeless to pursue.[3]

Merad presents his reflections on Charles de Foucauld as a contribution to this dialogue. His message has lessons not only for the few who are actively engaged in the field of Christian-Muslim relations, but also for the many who could, and should, be drawn into the conversation.

## Charles de Foucauld[4]

Charles de Foucauld was born in Strasbourg in 1858, into an ancient noble family, originally from the Périgord, that over the centuries had furnished France with soldiers, courtiers and priests. Orphaned at the age of six, he and his sister were sent to live with their maternal grandfather, an elderly retired colonel who tended to indulge the headstrong boy. He was intelligent but lazy, and his academic record was unimpressive. When he decided on a military career, he chose St. Cyr because it had the easiest examination.

As a young cavalry officer, Foucauld led the life of a dissipated dandy. Corpulent and vain, with a taste for fine clothes and good food, he enjoyed gambling parties, lived openly with a mistress and ran through a fortune. He had long since lost his faith.

Nevertheless, even in this profligate period of his life there were indications of his natural gifts. As a lieutenant in the Fourth African Hussars, he proved to be a brave leader and was well liked by his men to whom he was devoted. He fought in Morocco and Algeria, an experience that left him with a lifelong passion for Africa and especially for the space, solitude and silence of the desert.

In 1883 he volunteered to go on a secret expedition to explore Morocco, a country then closed to the outside world. Guided by an eccentric rabbi, Charles de Foucauld traveled disguised as a Jew. With his surveying instruments concealed under his clothes, he managed to record astro-nomical and geographical date as well as notes on the life and customs of the people. His widely acclaimed book *Reconnaissance au Maroc*, which earned him a gold medal from the French National Geographic Society, demonstrated courage and powers of endurance together with the superb quality of scientific observation and analysis that character-ized his later work.

The encounter with Islam in North Africa had a profound effect on the young Frenchman. He was impressed by Muslims' constant repetition of the name of God, their pros-trations in prayer in the open desert and the haunting call of the muezzin. There is some evidence that at one time he was drawn to Islam himself. According to his biographer Bazin, Foucauld told friends that he had thought of becoming a Muslim. He admitted that Islam had disturbed him deeply, and that "the sight of this faith, of these souls living in the con-tinuous presence of God, has made me aware of something greater and more true than worldly preoccupations."[5] At the very least, this experience made him see the emptiness of his life and prompted him to undertake his own spiritual journey.

On his return to France in 1886, Foucauld suffered from bouts of melancholy and an "infinite sense of boredom." At this crisis in his life, he met Abbé Huvelin. The scholarly priest, a gifted spiritual director with a reputation for holiness, was to provide him with wise and tactful guidance through the vicissitudes of the years ahead. When Foucauld sought instruction, Abbé Huvelin told him to kneel down and confess his sins and he would believe. The future at once became clear. He later described his reaction to a friend: "The moment I realized that God existed, I knew that I could not do otherwise than live for Him alone; my religious vocation dates from the same moment as my faith."[6]

On the advice of Abbé Huvelin, Foucauld made a pilgrimage to the Holy Land. When he returned, he was admitted, at the age of thirty-two, to the Trappist monastery of Our Lady of the Snows. He soon became known for his extreme austerities. He once explained his need for mortification in these revealing words: "When you want to write on a blackboard, you must begin by rubbing out what has been written there. I am always busy rubbing out."[7]

In 1891 he asked to be transferred to Akbès in Syria, the poorest and most remote house of the order. There he continued with his rigorous fasts and vigils and worked barefoot in the fields. Yet even this harsh existence failed to give him what he was looking for. When permission was granted to introduce oil and butter into the kitchen, Foucauld complained in a letter to his cousin: "Where will this end? On what slippery slope have we started? This is not the poverty I desired, the abjection of which I dreamed; on this score my desires are not satisfied."[8] After seven years as a Trappist, he was released from his vows to follow his special vocation.

From 1897 to 1900, calling himself Brother Charles of Jesus, Foucauld worked as an unpaid servant at a convent of the Poor

Clares, first in Nazareth and then in Jerusalem. Dressed like a beggar, he slept in a garden shed with a stone for a pillow. Apart from his simple tasks, he led a solitary life of silence, prayer and contemplation. He wrote: "Lord Jesus, how quickly will he be poor, he who, loving you with all his heart, cannot abide being richer than his beloved master!"⁹ So began the imitation of Jesus that was to be his ideal for the rest of his life.

He finally yielded to encouragement to enter the priesthood and was ordained in France in 1901. Then, drawn by an "irresistible urge," he set off for Algeria and settled in the lonely, poverty-stricken oasis of Béni-Abbès. With the help of soldiers from the nearby French garrison, he built a small hermitage and chapel of mud bricks and palm branches. His days were devoted to charity, manual work, study and prayer. He lived on bread, water and a handful of dates and slept at the foot of the altar, "curled up like a dog at the feet of his Master."¹⁰

Despite the peace and happiness of life in his enclosure at Béni-Abbès, in 1905 Charles de Foucauld moved south into the desert at the invitation of his old friend Colonel Laperrine, commander in chief of the Saharan oases. He finally came to rest in Tamanrasset, "a god-forsaken village in the heart of the Hoggar mountains, the home of the Tuareg."¹¹

These legendary blue-veiled warriors were the most warlike of all the desert tribes. Addicted to raiding and feuding, they were known to the French for their cunning and treachery. In 1889, they were responsible for the massacre of the expedition under Colonel Flatters that checked the French advance for more than twenty years. It was not until the Battle of Tit (1902) that the seemingly invincible "lords of the desert" were finally defeated by modern firepower.

Of a mysterious origin, supposedly descended from the ancient Libyans, the Tuareg were tall, well built and fair-skinned. Foucauld compared them to the Egyptians in ancient sculptures. With their hide tents, camel and goat herds, they led a pastoral existence. Although poor nomads, they were a proud people with a deep suspicion of outsiders, and they regarded the French as pagans and savages.

These were to be Charles de Foucauld's neighbors for the rest of his life, the "mistrustful brothers" whom he set out to "tame." He settled down in his little hermitage of stones and mud and began to study their language, working indefatigably through the years to compile the first Tamashegh grammar and dictionary. In the end, the Tuareg said that he knew their tongue better than they did. He became an authority on their history and collected and transcribed their proverbs, poetry and traditional folklore.

With his knowledge of Tuareg language and customs, Foucauld was a fount of information for the army. As a keen patriot and erstwhile soldier, he maintained close links with the regional command, sending reports on the political situation to Laperrine by monthly courier. He had, by this time, become almost unrecognizable to his former fellow officers. He was now an emaciated figure clad in a ragged white robe, with a red heart crowned by a cross stitched on his breast. His feet were bare and his hands deeply cut and bruised by toil. All that remained of the old Foucauld were his fine eyes, sweet smile and the rare charm that captivated men and women from all walks of life: monks in France and Syria, wounded soldiers whom he tended and befriended in Algeria, a Protestant doctor who stayed with him in Tamanrasset, the French officers who idolized him and, finally, the Tuareg.

His only link with the outside world was the military camp at In-Salah, over four hundred miles away. Yet despite this solitary life, Foucauld was no recluse. In line with his own advice that "you have to take the first step," he set out to befriend people, making contact with his wary neighbors and winning them over with his gentle manner. As "universal brother" he entered into their concerns, laughed and played

with the children, cared for the sick and the poor and dispensed simple hospitality to a constant stream of visitors.

The amenukal[12] Moussa ag Amastane, a man who had
earned the trust and respect of the French, became a valued
friend whom Charles de Foucauld admired and counseled
over the years. Later, when the Tuareg chief heard of the
death of the hermit, he wrote in a touching letter to
Foucauld's sister in France: "Charles the marabout has
died not only for you, he has died for us too. May God have
mercy on him, and may we meet him in Paradise."[13]

Driven to seek ever greater hardship and seclusion, in 1910
Charles de Foucauld built a crude stone hermitage at
Assekrem on the summit of the mountain, nearly ten thou-
sand feet above sea level. There he spent three months of the
year. The site was so inaccessible that it took several days to
reach it and he had to equip himself with crates of provisions
and books as if embarking on a sea voyage. It was a setting of
stark beauty, surrounded by tall columns of rock in strange
formations, a fine spot, he said to worship the Creator.

Earlier, Foucauld had written: "It is so pleasant and so
healthy to set oneself down in solitude, face to face with the
eternal things; one feels oneself penetrated by the truth."[14]
Silent upon his peak in Assekrem, he had finally found a
place that satisfied this lifelong yearning for solitude. At the
same time it brought him closer to his "dear parishioners,"
Tuareg who were fleeing from the drought. Nomad families
from the surrounding valleys made the rocky ascent to the
hermitage to visit the Christian marabout and to share his
humble fare while they watched the sunset together.

The end of this remarkably full and varied life came
abruptly. Within months of the outbreak of the First World
War, the region was stirred up by the contending parties. Law
and order broke down and raiders roamed the countryside.
Charles de Foucauld, choosing to stay with his people, took
refuge in a small fort that he had designed as a haven for the

inhabitants of Tamanrasset in case of attack. On December 1, 1916, they were set upon by an armed band that had learned of their store of food and munitions. The plan seems to have been to seize the booty and take the hermit hostage. In the confusion, a boy left to guard him panicked and shot him by mistake. According to an eyewitness, Charles de Foucauld died swiftly and in silence.

The general view has been that the raiders were Sanusi,[15] members of the Libyan reforming order that had long fought against the European expansion in North Africa. Merad, however, maintains that despite their hostility to the French, the Sanusi brotherhood regarded it as their duty to respect Christians, especially priests. He views the attack at Tamanrasset as one of many episodes in that turbulent and anarchic time.

At all events, Charles de Foucauld's life ended in apparent failure. He had made no converts and he left no successors. His rule of life for a new religious order existed only on paper.[16] He died as he had lived, alone, a death that was not even a martyrdom.

In a letter to a friend, he wrote: "I am preparing the ground, others will sow, others will reap."[17] The words proved to be prophetic. A group of young priests were inspired by his spiritual writings, the biblical simplicity of his life and "the death in the desert, the prayer in forgotten places."[18] They responded to the appeal of a religious vocation that could be pursued living among the masses and teaching by example.

The order of the Little Brothers of Jesus was founded in 1933 and the Little Sisters of Jesus followed six years later. Today, throughout the world, there are small "fraternities" whose lives bear witness to their faith. Unlike the traditional contemplative orders, they make their home among the poor and the disadvantaged, working alongside them as dockers, miners, fishermen and shoemakers. True to their spiritual heritage, they continue to maintain a permanent presence in

Tamanrasset and Assekrem, where they are still regarded with affection by the Tuareg of the Hoggar.

Charles de Foucauld's valiant attempt to "cry the Gospel" with his life left a profound mark on Christian spirituality. It also deeply affected a distinguished Muslim scholar, Ali Merad, and moved him to write this very personal tribute.

# Christian Hermit in an Islamic World

## A Muslim's View of Charles de Foucauld

Whosoever obeys God, and the Messenger—
they are with those whom God has blessed,
Prophets, just men, martyrs, the righteous;
good companions, they!

Quran, IV, 69.

# Preface

WHY YET ANOTHER BOOK ABOUT CHARLES DE FOUCAULD? There are already a number of good studies dedicated to the Hermit of the Sahara. Some of them go back thirty years and to a certain extent reflect the outlook and atmosphere of the colonial era. There are more recent ones that set out to dust off the legendary figure of the Little Brother of Jesus in order to restore the pure, unvarnished truth.

In this abundant literature, Christian inspiration quite naturally predominates. It would be hard to find a book on Charles de Foucauld that represents the testimony of a Muslim. Is there a lack of interest in this man of God, this mystical flame that flared in the desert? Or indifference to his impassioned—and still relevant—message? Or ignorance of his true importance in modern Christian spirituality? It is hardly conceivable. Are there then reservations? We will try below to point to the reasons for the Islamic silence on the subject of the extraordinary destiny of a man who devoted his life to bearing witness to Jesus before the Muslim community, to prepare the terrain for the seed of the Gospel in the land of Islam.

This little book in no way claims to provide an Islamic answer (still less *the* Islamic answer) to the "case" of Charles de Foucauld. Neither does it constitute an "essay" produced along the lines of university research. It does not wish to demonstrate or prove anything at all. It seeks neither to jus⁄tify nor to condemn.

It is simply the testimony of a man who, at a certain moment in time (and this goes back more than twenty years), felt himself summoned by to message of Charles de Foucauld, and who, many times since then, has pondered on the significance—for Islam—of this Christian life implanted on the heart of an Islamic land.

It is, therefore, an act of testimony. More specifically, it is a testimony motivated by the desire to make a contribution, however small, to the Muslim⁄Christian dialogue. By that we mean a dialogue that should not be restricted to pleasantries and the courtesies of respect and mutual tolerance, but which should aim to promote the necessary reciprocal understanding, based on as clear a knowledge as possible of the respective problems. This dialogue should make use of all written and oral sources of information, and have as its constant concern a greater insight into the feelings, ideas and doctrines that form, on both sides, the foundations of faith and culture.

In this light, it is urgent to surmount the age⁄old barriers, maintained by mistrust and prejudice, and weighed down with grievances accumulated in the course of a long histori⁄cal process marked by relations of force and domination.

The whole Arab nation is free politically and on the way to economic freedom, now that Islam has regained full inde⁄pendence in its traditional geo⁄political and cultural area. Nothing then really stands in the way of new bonds being formed between Christians and Muslims, bonds that go beyond assumptions, accusations and condemnations on both sides, in a climate of politico⁄cultural confrontation that no longer has any reason to exist.

At this point, we both ought calmly to approach the exam⁄ination of the problems that have set us against each other, or divided us in the course of history. Is it really still necessary to prepare for battle armed with an outdated polemic? Does it make any sense to draw up an indictment of doctrinal attitudes and positions, framed in a socio-cultural logic peculiar to the generation of 1880 to 1910, and to do this in terms of the political criteria and cultural categories of our age?

It is essential, we think, neither to approve nor to condemn the actions and conduct of a man like the great "Christian marabout" of the Sahara, a man who was, for better or worse, rooted in the political context of his time. Have not the lives of many Muslim saints had political and social effects that have been deemed glorious or deplorable, according to the point of view of the different parties involved?

What man, however admirable the holiness of his life, has not found himself tempted, at some time, to play the role of "wonder-worker" in the social and political order? But mystics—like idealistic reformers—have rarely been political "wonders." They have generally lacked the authority essential to realize their moral and political aims. And when, by some miracle, they have for a time had access to decision-making power, it has generally ended in failure, for want of political sense, realism, savoir faire and at times even Machiavellianism. Without these qualities the noblest intentions can never be translated into concrete reality in the world, in terms of effective and lasting reforms.

Besides, should errors of judgment and organization, which in politicians would be considered minor matters, be necessarily regarded as unpardonable crimes in the case of men of God? It was through his wish to serve his fellow men, no doubt too well (and perhaps too quickly), that Charles de Foucauld found himself enmeshed in temporal affairs for which he had no more aptitude than anyone else.

A holy fool is first and foremost a man. And so was Charles de Foucauld: a person consumed by an inner fire that was, for him, the love of Jesus and a passion for the imitation of Jesus.

But this person was no less a man, that is, a Frenchman of the end of the nineteenth century, shaped by his education and the culture of his time as well as by his military training and, what is more, locked into the framework of colonialism, a factor that needs careful consideration.

A good alibi, you may say. Is not an authentic saint the man who rejects every kind of conformity and system and invents his own values in order to inaugurate a new order, without the support of—and if necessary counter to—the established order? This sort of argument assumes that sanctity necessarily fosters a revolutionary spirit. It is true that the culture of our time highly values—and tends at times even to sanctify—revolutionary fervor. The concept of revolution is often invested with the noblest values of classical humanism: generosity, intellectual courage and passionate commitment to liberty and the dignity of man. As a result, men and ideas are blithely judged according to over-simplified criteria of "revolution" and "reaction," as if nothing important had happened in human history apart from crises and upheavals on the scale of civilizations and empires.

However, many socio-cultural and political changes have been initiated by patient work carried out at grass-roots level by ordinary men who had no ambition to change the face of the world, but who tirelessly sowed the good seed, conscious that they were preparing for future harvests.

To refer only to Muslim history: There is the example of two reformers who stirred Muslim consciousness toward the end of the nineteenth century and whose moral and doctrinal influence is still felt today; they are: the Iranian Afghan Jamāl al-Dīn al-Afghānī (died in 1897) and the Egyptian Muhammad Abduh (died in 1905). The former advocated ideological struggle and dramatic action simultaneously against British imperialism and despotic Muslim national regimes, in order to hasten the political, social and cultural liberation of the Muslim people. Muhammad Abduh's doctrine was quite

the reverse. He preached the moral regeneration and socio-
cultural restoration of the Muslim world by peaceful means:
the spread of education, the popularization of science and
modern technology, and the education of public opinion by
both written and oral propaganda. It was Muhammad
Abduh's approach that in the end triumphed almost everywhere, so that from Morocco to Indonesia, the Muslim world
venerates the memory of the great Egyptian thinker and hails
him as the true father of the Islamic renaissance in modern
times. No one today would dream of blaming Muhammad
Abduh for having opposed his master al-Afghānī and for not
having adopted his "revolutionary" way.

Is it fair, then, to hold it against Charles de Foucauld for
not being ahead of his time, for not having somehow invented
political concepts that were, three quarters of a century
later, to become the leading concepts in contemporary political thought, and for not having managed to prophesy the
end of the colonial empires? This sort of reproach is unrea-
sonable and in the end unjust, in view of the social and cultural conditions—and the dominant political ideologies—of
the time.

One might as well regret that Pope Leo XIII was unable to
formulate the social doctrine of the Church in the encyclical
"Rerum Novarum" (1891), in terms comparable to those
adopted by John XXIII in his encyclical "Mater et Magistra"
(1961). One might, in the same way, deplore that this influen-
tial "native chief" or that renowned marabout behaved,
around 1900–1915, for example, as an "objective ally" of the
colonial regime, and was incapable of transcending the outlook of his century to pose the Algerian problem in terms not
of simple "reforms," but of national liberation.

These remarks should not be taken as special pleading. It
must be repeated that there is no question of justifying anyone
or of promoting some new thesis about Charles de Foucauld.
We seek above all to understand. An undertaking such as this

involves a concern for intellectual integrity and requires, where necessary, that perspectives be correctly restored.

We seek then to show how this remarkable Christian presence in the land of Islam can be perceived by a Muslim. For the presence of Charles de Foucauld among the Tuareg of the Sahara was like a great question mark standing out against the horizon of the desert. Some would say that this presence constituted a kind of challenge for Islam. We prefer to speak of a summons. A living summons. One can say no more.

Islam therefore has good reason for asking how to make sense of this summons. No doubt some Muslims would quite simply impugn such a summons and reject its implications in advance. Others would consider that they have a right to reflect on the sign named: Charles de Foucauld.

This is what we have tried to do in the following pages. It is a view of Charles de Foucauld offered by someone who wishes to remain calm and collected, and is unencumbered with vain political categories when it comes to the consideration of an entire life directed toward an ideal of holiness and brotherly love.

# I

# *Happiness in the imitation of Jesus*

FOR A MUSLIM TO EMBARK on an investigation of the life and work of a saintly Christian may appear unusual, even somewhat presumptuous. And when, with all the will in the world, the Muslim observer is restricted to academic information, comprehensive as it may be, as his sole source, how can he hope to arrive at a real understanding of a spirituality that is not his own? Even if he were equipped with all the desired erudition, he would lack that inner knowledge, sustained by religious feeling and the communion of minds, without which it would be idle to claim a sound understanding of a man and his message.

But in the case of a person like Charles de Foucauld, a Christian missionary in the land of Islam, who chose to live—and to die—close to, if not in the very heart of, the Muslim community, the view of a Muslim should not be regarded as indiscreet. This is especially so when that view is not motivated by purely intellectual curiosity, what Louis Massignon calls that "secular mania to understand,"[1] but by a sincere desire to grasp, through the extraordinary life of this man of God, the signs that reveal the work of the spirit in the course of human history.

More specifically, in our case, there is in addition to this inner impulse arising from the attraction of holiness, the desire to reflect on the meaning for a Muslim, and, for Islam in general, of the example of Charles de Foucauld, viewed as a missionary monk and servant of his brothers, the men of the desert.

In fact, it is not our aim to produce a comprehensive appreciation of the life and work of Charles de Foucauld. (Would such an undertaking by a Muslim even be permissible?) So much has been written on the "Hermit of the Sahara," "the Apostle of the Tuareg," that pays tribute to his civilizing work and his missionary activity, that one more attempt of this kind would seem superfluous.

But reading the numerous biographies that set out to idealize the figure of Charles de Foucauld, in which pious apologia for the Little Brother of Jesus lies side by side with moving evocations of the great servant of the French colonial enterprise in Africa, there is the sense of an indefinable void. Beside this rich literature of Christian origin, it seemed to us that there should be a place for an Islamic reflection on the work of Charles de Foucauld. For, on the one hand, this work directly concerned a Muslim population and, on the other, he himself took note of the Islamic factor in the conception and expression of his views.

We would like to pursue this reflection free from all reference to historical contingencies and ideological considerations. Ideologies are transient, as are the regimes that fuel them with the passions and blood of men. But beyond passing historical contingencies and human passions, there is the unchanging face of holiness; there are spiritual masters whose names sing out for all generations, like the eternal music of the wind and sea; there are lives that shine forever in the firmament of the centuries; there are messages that repeatedly summon humankind, beyond the diversity of belief and culture.

Charles de Foucauld belongs to this world of irreplaceable figures. He spoke to men, to Christians and to Muslims, in the language of the Gospel. Although he carried out his apostolate among them in exclusive fidelity to the word and life of Jesus Christ, Muslims were not unmoved by his evangelical virtues and did not seek to deter him in his work of spiritual "taming."

There are so many things that could be said about the encounter between Charles de Foucauld and Islam, not simply social Islam, but Islam envisaged as a revelation and a living culture. We will refrain from alluding to grievances that would be easy to formulate, from the Muslim point of view, when considering aspects of Charles de Foucauld's public activity in line with French colonial policy, and some of his judgments or attitudes toward the phenomenon of Islam. In this connection, his "Ecrits Spirituels," as well as the testimony of his contemporaries, provide documentary evidence that is very informative.

But what concerns us at present is the image of a man who renounced everything, his fondest affections, the attractions of the world, the advantages of wealth and the gratifying prospect of a fine career, to dedicate himself totally to the service of the lowly, in a distant land where he felt he would be able to imitate the example of Jesus more perfectly. For he regarded the imitation of Jesus as his greatest happiness and, even more, as his true raison d'être. This imitation of Jesus by Charles de Foucauld will constitute the central theme of our reflection.

To imitate Jesus, to strive at all times to act as he himself would have done; to treat each person as "not a man, but Jesus" (ECR.SPIR., 211), is, from the Muslim point of view, the most eloquent way to espouse the authenticity of the Gospel message.

To draw a parallel, it should be pointed out that, in the case of Islam, the imitation of the Prophet (Muhammad) is regarded as the true sign of faith and the best response to the call of God (cf. Quran, XXXIII,21: "You have had a good example in God's Messenger for whosoever hopes for God and the Last Day, and remembers God oft"). Thus the great Algerian reformer (and commentator of the Quran) Ibn Bādis (1889–1940) stated in a famous saying the principle that "the more perfect the imitation of the Prophet, the more perfect is the fulfillment of the mission to call on God."[2]

In the same way, the perfect imitation of Jesus by a Christian must assume a great moral and spiritual significance in the eyes of Muslims. It is a way of responding to the Islamic expectation of "People of the Book," who are only fully recognized as such—and so accepted as "valid interlocutors"—insofar as they prove themselves completely faithful to their respective Scriptures.

In this connection, it is good to meditate on the Quranic summons addressed to Christians: "Let the People of the Gospel judge according to what God has sent down therein" (V,47). It should be noted that this verse does not allude to the practice of justice. The concept of ḥukm, in ancient Arabic, includes both the idea of the legal description of an act (one that gives rise to a verdict following arbitration), and that of moral judgment. The latter is understood not as the expression of a simple, somewhat arbitrary personal opinion, but as the fruit of reflection that is firmly grounded and wholeheartedly embraced.

The Quran seems to indicate that the Gospel is *the* supreme criterion for Christians and their fundamental source of reference. So it is to a return to the values of the Gospel that Christians find themselves invited by this Quranic appeal. Such a return involves a greater fidelity, on their part, to the divine message revealed there. In this light, Charles de Foucauld's life is a fine illustration of the desire to return—and of fidelity—to the Gospel. Thus conspicuous among men should be "those who say 'We are Christians'" (Quran, V, 82), and who truly wish to be so *(innā naṣārā).*

The figure of Charles de Foucauld corresponds in yet another way to the expectation of those Muslims who tend to judge Christian attitudes not only in themselves but also in relation to the Quranic statements about Christianity. The great lesson that emerges from the solitary, silent life of Charles de Foucauld is his humility, his gentleness and his charity. One of his resolutions (during the retreat in 1902 at Béni-Abbès): "Always to be humble, gentle and helpful, as Jesus, Mary and Joseph were in the Holy House at Nazareth.—Gentleness, humility, abjection, charity: to serve others" (ECR.SPIR., 210). It is in very similar terms that the Quran describes the true disciples of Christ as those in whose hearts God set "tenderness and mercy" (LVII,27), and who "wax not proud" (V,82).

Humility, charity, the renunciation of the pleasures and good things of this world and devotion to the service of the poor and unfortunate are virtues that have always strongly impressed Muslims, conscious as they are of the sacrifice involved for Europeans. It is fair to say that this feeling was shared equally by ordinary people and by religious leaders (marabouts, *'ulamā'*), and even by reformist elements (defenders of "Arab-Muslim nationalism"), who generally took a stern view of anything that recalled the system or ethos of colonialism.

We have examined elsewhere[3] the attitude of the reformers toward the Catholic Church in Algeria, and shown that the founders of the Algerian reform movement never allowed themselves to be drawn into an anti-Christian or anti-Catholic polemic. Their only grievances against the Church reflected indignant reactions to some tactless move by the local clergy which they found hurtful to the pride of Muslims and hostile to Islam.[4] For this reason, one does not find in reformist writings of the period between the two wars

any systematic endeavor to refute Christianity or to combat
the moral and social influence of Christian missionaries. On
the contrary, in many reformist writers of the period, one
detects a certain admiration for the charity and spirit of sacrifice of most missionaries, and even a cautious sympathy for
the Church, insofar as it symbolized for them cohesiveness
and harmonious discipline.

Thus the reformers did not seek to deny the grandeur of
Christian missionary work in the land of Islam. In this context, it is useful to recall the testimony of Shakīb Arslān
(1869–1946), a man of letters, publicist and patriot of Libyan
extraction (nicknamed at the time "The Prince of Elo-
quence"), who was, in matters of Arabism, the true intellectual
leader of the Algerian reformers, as well as of the entire first
Arab generation of the twentieth century. Shakīb Arslān pays
tribute to Catholic and Protestant missionaries in these
words: "I have the greatest respect for these people, and I wish
that among Muslims there were men capable of accomplishing
only a tenth of their sacrifices in the service of their community.—For these men the interests of colonialism count as
nothing beside the propagation of the Christian faith, which is
their supreme objective.—Where then are the Muslim missionaries ready to sacrifice material prosperity, traverse
deserts, scale mountains, and cross oceans, for the sole purpose of spreading the word of Monotheism?"[5]

The feelings that Muslims entertained toward Christian
monks were generally characterized by esteem if not genuine
friendship. Muslims acknowledged that these monks represented a certain image of Christianity and were faithful, in
their way, to the message of Jesus Christ. This favorable pre-
sumption was heightened among Muslims by the view that
monks form, within the so-called Christian nations, a sort of
"community apart" (to use Quranic terminology), a community of men working for the spread of Good and the elimina-
tion of Evil, and believing in God (Quran, III, 110).

In fact, in the view of traditional Muslim society, Europe evoked not only Christianity, but also the idea of a humanity endowed with all the conditions for earthly happiness which, in thrall to the allurements of the world, was unmindful of its future destiny.[6] For people used to the rough, eventful life of the desert or the monotonous life of the oasis, where hardship and disease were the common lot, the European was regarded as a privileged being, normally able to aspire to every assurance of happiness.

When this European man or woman, when these Christians, gave up their advantages and chose to come and share the wretched lot of the Muslim population in the mountains or the desert, such a choice must have appeared to be the outcome of a conversion bearing the unmistakable mark of the divine.

Hence, the signs of respect, trust and affection with which the Tuareg surrounded their venerable neighbor, the "Christian marabout."

This led the latter to say: "My Tuareg friends are comforting and affectionate; on this score, I am happy" (GOR., p. 264).

Hence the compassionate words of the great amenukal of the Hoggar, Moussa ag Amastane, on his return from a journey to France (summer 1910), in the course of which he had met Charles de Foucauld's family: "I saw your sister," he wrote as soon as he disembarked at Algiers (September 10). "I also saw your brother-in-law; I visited their gardens and their homes. And there you are in Tamanrasset, like a pauper!" (BAZ, p. 393). This laconic and touching phrase expresses all the affectionate admiration and tender feeling possible for a rough warrior like the Tuareg chief.

# II

# *An ideal of holiness*

A S A "CHRISTIAN MARABOUT" IN THE LAND OF ISLAM, Charles de Foucauld introduced the Muslim community to a very different idea of holiness from the one familiar to them in the context of traditional maraboutism. There was, of course, a difference in appearance and language between Charles de Foucauld and a local marabout, in addition to the difference in religious inspiration. But the fundamental disparity was in the sphere of human relations. And it is this point that deserves particular attention.

Without seeking to do a psycho-sociological analysis of Algerian maraboutism at the time of Charles de Foucauld, it may be useful to recall some of the general features that characterized the social relations of the marabout chiefs and their simple followers. At the time that concerns us (the end of the nineteenth and beginning of the twentieth century), the social and personal relations of the master-marabout ("Sheikh")[1] with each of his disciples were governed by a code of traditions and customs that involved honor as much as faith. Furthermore, these relations took place, on both sides, under the sign of the sacred, so that any lapse or non-observance assumed the proportions of an act of treason, if not a crime.

The Sheikh had an indisputable moral right over his disciples and followers. In some circumstances, the "moral right" amounted to a pious euphemism. Hence the extraordinary influence most marabouts had over the faithful and the rule of strict allegiance that bound the latter to the former. This allegiance was expressed in daily life by a subservient, reverential attitude and by actions that embodied devotion and total submission to the sheikh: It entailed being available at all times, eager to satisfy—or to anticipate—the smallest desires of the master and swift to carry out his orders, including the most capricious; all in the secret hope of earning his trust and attracting his blessings, or at least of escaping his wrath and his curse, for what was dreaded most of all was the curse of the master-marabout.

The range and consequences of this curse are detailed in popular traditions and have spawned an exuberant and truly terrifying literature. The testimony and authority of personages noted for their great virtue and piety gave weight to legends that were presented as true "slices of life." These legends, that formed an integral part of popular religion, perpetuated a belief in the "miracles" performed by various spiritual masters and in the punishment of former followers for rebelliousness or disloyalty. There were horror stories calculated to fire the imagination of simple souls and make the sensitive shudder: degrading metamorphoses, physical defects and incurable diseases (especially paralyses), the ruin and breakup of families, and so on. In these tales, the outline emerges of a veritable code of threats worked out in maraboutic circles, designed to persuade people that the spiritual masters were beings possessed of supernatural powers. Through these powers they were able at any moment—and wherever they might be—to strike the skeptical or the disobedient, the underhanded or the wayward, in a word all who sought to challenge the marabouts. This would include those who renounced their oath and broke the sacred bond, either to go over to a rival brotherhood or to free themselves completely from all obedience to marabouts.[2]

The maraboutic relationship was not only characterized by the unconditional submission of followers to their master. There was also the ceremonial and ritual order that regulated all the words and actions of the marabout in the presence of the faithful. On the occasion of mass visits or the celebration of religious festivals, the appearance of the sheikh was almost always a solemn act, rather like an impressive dramatic performance. At these times, marabouts readily adopted a hieratic pose, as if to affirm their detachment from the common condition of simple mortals and their affinity for a kind of superhuman (if not supernatural) world. In addition, they usually strove hard to maintain an air of mystery about themselves: few of the intimates or elect were admitted to the secrets of their private life or to confidences about their thoughts or plans. The mass of the faithful had to be satisfied with a perpetual, intoxicating uncertainty on this side of the sacred veil (ḥijāb) that had necessarily to separate the secular world from the ineffable mysteries of holiness.

Thus the marabouts were able to escape the appeals and possible familiarities of their followers, and at the same time to inspire the latter with reverential awe before the "friends of God" (awliyāʾ, plural of walī) and the "receivers of the divine." In these circumstances, to approach the marabout, albeit fleetingly, was experienced as a privilege and a piece of exceptional good fortune.

*        *        *

This brief digression into the field of Algerian maraboutism was necessary to give some idea of the novelty represented by Charles de Foucauld's example in a Muslim setting that was profoundly affected by maraboutic influence.[3] The solitary Brother of Béni-Abbès, the hermit of Tamanrasset, offered Muslims the image of a man of God without ceremony and without predilection for mystery or pretension to supernatural power. The holiness he sought to espouse was active and

down to earth, and did not in any way aim to confer salvation
miraculously by the sole means of presence and contact.

Far be it from us to set up a systematic contrast between
maraboutism and the way chosen by Charles de Foucauld.
Among the marabouts, there were certainly men devoted to
simplicity and, like him, concerned with practical effective⁄
ness—in the service of their fellows—in everyday life. But
these were, in general, men of God who sprang from the
popular community, and who made no claims to the nobility
or religious aristocracy that was the boast of the majority of
marabouts with their flattering, if somewhat hypothetical,
genealogies.

On the other hand, the heads of the great maraboutic
houses, the regional representatives of the grand Muslim
orders (like the Qādiriya, the Shādhiliya, the Tījāniya), felt
obliged to maintain a distance between themselves and the
people that was doubtless judged necessary out of respect for
their office and the prestige of their rank. They were careful, of
course, to see to it that their *zāwāya*,[4] as far as possible, carried
out the functions of education, hospitality and charity. But
their own role was to promote the salvation of souls by the
blessings that they distributed and the power of intercession
with which they believed themselves to be invested.

In accordance with this conception, all duties and serv⁄
ices were their due. The rank of marabout conferred a social
status that was unique of its kind. Since they were spiritual
masters, patrons and nobles all at the same time, the entire
community of the faithful was theoretically subject to them.
It is significant that followers of the maraboutic brother⁄
hoods defined themselves first and foremost as humble ser⁄
vants *(khuddām)* of the master⁄marabout.

Charles de Foucauld's attitude was totally different. He
had chosen to adopt the position of the humble, the little
people. "My aim is always to seek the very lowest place, to be
as lowly as my Master, to be with Him, to walk behind Him,

in his footsteps, as a faithful servant, a faithful disciple..."
(ECR.SPIR., 56). Thus instead of relying on the work of
others, he joyfully embraced "manual work and holy
poverty" (ECR.SPIR., 204).

In the case of simple people, as were the great majority of
the Saharan population, the example of the Christian
marabout tended to strengthen their regard for the nobility
and holiness of manual work. Most marabouts readily
excused themselves from all manual activity, arguing the
privileges of their calling. This was the case particularly with
the Shurfa [shurafā] marabouts who claimed descent from
the Prophet and constituted a sort of religious aristocracy
able to exercise comprehensive rights over the faithful: all
sorts of corvées (in particular in the field of agricultural
work), donations in kind, financial contributions at visits
(ziyāra) and festivals, etc. On the other hand, they did not
feel bound to their followers by any obligations other than
those that suited them or met their concern to safeguard
their authority and prestige with the masses.

Breaking with these medieval-like practices and over-
turning regulations based on the force of custom, Charles de
Foucauld affirmed his vocation as servant "marabout," in
contrast to the traditional image of the marabout for whom
all the faithful were essentially servants. Among his resolutions (1902, Béni-Abbès): "To get rid of the orderly:[5] to
serve, not to be served" (ECR.SPIR., 213). Devotion to the
service of men, the will for self-abasement, descent and
humility in order to serve men better: these are constant
themes in Charles de Foucauld's "Ecrits Spirituels."

These themes do not merely reflect generous ideas or
purely theoretical resolutions. The "Universal Brother" dis-
played great zeal in the service of the Saharans who came to
see him, or whom he met in the course of his rounds through
the oases and ksour of Saura, Touat and Guerara, or through
Tidikelt and the Hoggar. He devoted himself to alleviating

poverty and disease by distributing food and giving freely of
his care and remedies.[6]

Beyond these not insignificant social works, Charles de
Foucauld strove to perform the humblest services and did
not shrink from the most menial duties. One of his resolutions (Béni-Abbès, 1902): "To do the washing of the poor
(particularly on Holy Thursday) and to clean their rooms
regularly, as far as possible *myself*. To do, as far as possible
*myself* and no one else, all the lowest tasks in the house (...);
to undertake every kind of service, and to be like Jesus, who
was among the apostles 'the one who serves' (...). To cook for
the poor, when I can; to bring them food and drink, not to
leave this service to others ..." (ECR.SPIR.,210-211). These
words need no commentary. They admirably define the new
image of the man of God that the "Christian marabout" was
to embody, for fifteen years, in the heart of the Muslim community.

*       *       *

By his example, Charles de Foucauld certainly contributed, in Muslim eyes, to restoring a scale of values in the
true sense. The Islamicist will immediately recognize in the
teaching of the Little Brother of Jesus—as in his quest for
moral perfection—ideas that are in accord with the Quranic
revelation and the pure tradition of primitive Islam.

1.  Piety is not demonstrated exclusively in the contemplative life or in ritual observance. It is essentially active and
radiant, creating happiness and inspiring goodness in men.
This is a principle that is well established in Islamic doctrine.
On this subject, the Quran issues a solemn warning: "It is
not piety, that you turn your faces to the East and to the
West..." (II.177). There follow in detail the good works that go
to make up the Quranic definition of true piety: charity (to
the poor, the orphan, the solitary traveler, etc.), the ransom

of captives, respect for agreements, steadfastness in adver-
sity and misfortune, and in the face of danger.[7] "These," con-
tinues the Quran, "are they who are true in their faith, these
are the truly godfearing."

This same teaching is illustrated by the following anec-
dote, taken from the Tradition of the Prophet. "One day, in
the presence of the Prophet, some visitors praised the
exceptional piety—according to them—of one of their trav-
eling companions.

—He is a man who never ceases to invoke God the whole
time we are on the move; and when we come to a halt, he
does not cease saying his prayers until we set out again.

—And all the time he is praying, asked the Prophet, who
sees to the preparation of his food and the care of his mount?

—Why, we all do!

—Well then, replied the Prophet, you are all better men
than he."

2. A lesson can be drawn from the example of Charles de
Foucauld. Holiness is not the prerogative of a certain line-
age or social class. Men of God do not, as a consequence of
their spiritual vocation, cease to belong to the society of their
time. Rather their responsibilities are increased in both the
moral and the social sphere. Even if they assume the func-
tion of guides—cf. the Islamic concept of the *imām*[8]—in the
forefront of the spiritual movement of their time, they
remain nonetheless servants, profoundly involved in the
problems and misfortunes of the human condition, and
engaged—no doubt more intensely than anyone else—in the
patient effort of humanity to build a better world.

3. The example of Charles de Foucauld was thus well
suited to challenge traditional values in a Muslim setting.
Through contact with him, more than one sincere believer
among the inhabitants of the oases or the Tuareg was led to

wonder about the true message of this "Christian marabout," who seemed to have been raised up by Providence to embody once again some of the fundamental values of pure *islām*: wholehearted submission to God, simplicity and the quest for moral perfection, at the same time as the firm resolve to con-tribute—even in an obscure and modest way—to creating a society characterized by justice and brotherly love.

# III

# What does "taming" mean?

ACCORDING TO ALL THOSE WHO KNEW HIM WELL, either at Béni-Abbès or in the Hoggar, no one could remain indifferent to Charles de Foucauld. What was true for French soldiers trained in the rough school of the Saharan Companies was equally true for Saharan natives who had the chance to meet or visit him.

Unfortunately, we lack documentary evidence from Muslim sources, so that it is not easy to determine exactly how the Saharan people regarded Charles de Foucauld as a person. Nevertheless, a few letters from the Tuareg chief, Moussa ag Amastane, some personal notes of Charles de Foucauld (whom no one could ever suspect of complacency), and various accounts by French superior officers (like Laperrine and Niéger) give us a fairly accurate idea of the kind of feelings entertained by the Saharans for this Christian monk who lived in their midst.

From this sort of evidence, it appears that Charles de Foucauld succeeded in gaining the trust and respect of the Tuareg, a proud, austere people who were particularly diffi-cult to "tame." The simplicity of his manner, the gentleness of his speech, and his charity and great piety won many hearts. His honesty and sense of justice led to his being appointed at times as an arbitrator.[1] Given the moral author-ity and social influence wielded by the arbitrator (ḥakam) in traditional bedouin society, one has some idea of the extent to which the "Christian marabout" had been adopted by the Muslim community in which he lived.

This sort of adoption would certainly not have been possible had the Muslims not recognized in Charles de Foucauld, not only the intellectual and social attributes of the leader and arbitrator and the virtues belonging to the People of the Gospel, but also the capacity so valued in the Islamic world, to undertake what is fittingly known as the "Call to Good," that is, the mission to enjoin Good and forbid Evil, to use specifically Quranic terminology.[2]

Most of the saints in the land of Islam—especially in the Maghrib—have been recognized as such not simply as a result of their great piety and the attraction of their spiritual "way" (tarīqa), but because of their role as religious and social reformers, in the local community or on a larger scale, in response to the Quranic injunction to enjoin Good and forbid Evil (cf. the two fundamental references: Quran, III, 104 and 110).

It is a fact, we believe, that Charles de Foucauld fully embraced in the moral sphere, as well as in the sphere of action, a mission similar to this Call to Good preached by the Quran, and that he strove—insofar as he was able—to promote good works among men and to reform, as far as he could, the evil tendencies in human nature.

All the evidence agrees on this point. Father de Foucauld knew how to show, if need be, to both his Muslim interlocutors and his officer friends, the severity required of the good shepherd. "His tolerance and patience were measured," notes General Niéger (NIE., 195). He kept quiet in the presence of blunders, but "infringements of fundamental principles of morality made him fly off the handle. He would not allow them even in jest. These reactions were in contrast to his usual gentleness; they were violent; violent enough to

make the joker regret having gone too far even if it was
Laperrine who liked to tease him" (Ibid.).

We have just reviewed some of Charles de Foucauld's attitudes that were likely to make him attractive to Muslims. But
in reality, the relations between the latter and the French
missionary monk scarcely went beyond the bounds of
respectful friendship. The rapprochement, it seems, was not
total. There was a lack of warmth.[3]

We are well aware that neither Charles de Foucauld nor
his Tuareg friends tended to express their feelings without
reserve. A proud and arrogant race, the Tuareg were, in
addition, uncommunicative, especially in the presence of a
stranger. Their sense of nobility ruled out facile relation-
ships as well as the unrestrained expression of emotion.

On his side, the scholarly hermit of the Hoggar had too lofty
an idea of his mission to allow himself social relations that
could be regarded as trivial or too familiar, and consequently
not sufficiently dignified for a monk who aspired to be an apostle, teacher and agent of civilization, all at the same time.
Besides, his important scientific work left him little leisure and
curbed any desire for ties that were too personal.

Thus, to our knowledge, few well known Muslims really
fraternized with Charles de Foucauld, with the exception of
Moussa ag Amastane who, through force of circumstances,
was thrown together with his Christian neighbor in Tamanrasset for a long period. Even then, it must be said that in
this particular case the relations between the two men were
not always noted for excessive cordiality. Foucauld had certain misgivings about the great amenukal of the Hoggar.[4]

While acknowledging the remarkable qualities of the chief[5]
and praising his complete loyalty and absolute fidelity to his
commitments,[6] he charged him with a dubious morality and a
touch of greed and guile (cf. BAZ., 322). It seems, too, that
Charles de Foucauld's feelings for Moussa ag Amastane gradually changed as the Tuareg chief increased his sway and

sought to establish his influence in the Hoggar, particularly in the organization of order and justice, and by his efforts to promote Quranic studies through a *zāwiya* and a mosque at Tamanrasset.[7]

Charles de Foucauld could not view without apprehension efforts that were likely to revive Islamic faith and culture among the Tuareg, and to retain a group of tribes reputed to be ungovernable under firm and vigilant Muslim authority. The political successes of ag Amastane exasperated Charles de Foucauld all the more because his "friend" acted openly in complete independence of both the French military authorities and the Christian marabout. Now the latter had a tendency to want to "cocoon" Moussa ag Amastane, to envelop him in paternal solicitude which, in all likelihood, the great Tuareg chief found more of a nuisance than a real help.[8]

Furthermore, because of the political context, relations between the two men were somewhat ambiguous. Charles de Foucauld must have appeared to Moussa ag Amastane as a sort of superior whom it was important to handle with caution, and at the same time as a guest who had to be treated with all the deference due to a stranger and, even more, to a man of God. Should they, above all other considerations, honor him as a guest and refrain from according him any temporal authority? Or should they, on the contrary, class him with the representatives of French power— the military[9]—and consequently no longer feel bound to him by the sacred duties of hospitality? One can imagine the kind of questions the Tuareg could have asked about their "Christian marabout" whose social status must have appeared so indefinable.

The ambiguity lay in the sense of authority associated with Charles de Foucauld. Was it purely moral authority or rather an authority that was both moral and political? Should he be regarded as a Christian—a Nazarene (*nasrānī*)—and only that, or should he at the same time be considered as a

Frenchman, that is, a man closely associated with the foreign forces of occupation?

This ambiguity is apparent throughout the "advice" that de Foucauld lavished on the Tuareg chief of the Hoggar. In this advice there is kindness, but with a certain condescension; alongside the impartial counsel of the older man that he was, and the friend, there are something like veiled warnings, the political significance of which would not have escaped the perspicacity of the intelligent amenukal.[10]

All this, it seems, would serve to explain the lack of warmth and depth in the mutual relations of the Tuareg—starting with one of their most distinguished chiefs, Moussa ag Amastane—and Charles de Foucauld. The relative severity of the latter's opinion of the amenukal does not sufficiently take into consideration the difficult position of his friend, who found himself torn between his pledges of loyalty to the French authorities and a natural fidelity to his associates and co-religionists who had not yet surrendered to the French, or who, defeated by the latter, considered themselves temporarily dominated but not subdued.[11]

On his side, Moussa ag Amastane no doubt appreciated the services rendered by the "Christian marabout" to his dependents, kinsmen and allies in the Hoggar. But with the instinct of a warrior and the political experience of a tribal chief, he could not have underestimated the risks he would run from conspicuously friendly relations with the Christian foreigner, the friend of superior officers in charge of policing the desert and defending the "Southern front" of the Algerian Sahara.

\*    \*    \*

The sole reason for the preceding remarks is to give an account of the obstacles, both psychological and socio-cultural, that Charles de Foucauld must have encountered in his efforts to "tame" the Tuareg population. Up till now, there has been no mention of difficulties arising from religious concerns. But one must not be so naïve as to believe that the Tuareg were only "pagans" who were superficially Islamized, as the great hermit of the Hoggar seemed to think.[12]

Certainly the Tuareg, like their bedouin co-religionists of Arab stock, did not exhibit the most robust and fervent of faiths. Their extreme mobility in the immense desert and their remoteness from centers of Islamic culture ensured a lack of education that hardly allowed them to experience a religious life of any depth. An Algerian saying characterizes rather well the life of the bedouin population who were doomed to wander: 'rab hāha—lā dīn, lā rāha: "The bedouins Hāha (know) neither religion, nor rest." This definition would obviously apply to the Tuareg; the quality of their Islamic life was neither better nor worse than that of many other Muslim tribes in the southern fringes of the Maghrib, from the Atlantic to the Libyan desert.

But in the absence of scrupulous piety and a faith nourished by an active spirituality, the Tuareg adopted beliefs and rituals that corresponded more or less accurately to the norms and values of Muslim orthodoxy. One has only to leaf through "Poésies Touarègues," collected by Charles de Foucauld himself, to realize how much Tuareg thought was influenced by the omnipresence of the idea of God and constant fidelity to the tradition of the Prophet. The pre-eminence of the sacred and the sense of Islamic tradition in the Tuareg view of life are reflected even in purely profane poetry, with its dominant themes of travel, warlike feats and amorous relations.[13]

If the Tuaregs' outward behavior showed few signs of religious zeal, does that necessarily imply an absence of religious awareness and warrant a categorical pronouncement on the weakness of their Islamic identification? It is clear that their faith was reduced to essentials (to a mere semblance of their Muslim culture), but their attachment to these essentials was as deep as it was to the vital necessities (water, cattle, etc.) that made their existence possible in the arid zone, that realm of thirst and death.

It is possible that Charles de Foucauld was, like many others after him, a victim of appearances. As a good Cartesian, he may have been tempted to draw logical conclusions from his patient observations in the Sahara. No mystical outpourings, no elaborate ritual, few regular religious practices, no visible clergy, no guilt complex, the absence in individuals of a conscience tortured by sin: These are sufficient arguments to indicate a state of paganism, if not total barbarity.

Moreover, the more or less open hostility of the Tuareg—and the Saharan population in general—to the progress of French expansion meant that natural defensive reactions in the presence of the foreign conqueror were reinforced by resistance movements in the traditional form of the "infidel." Charles de Foucauld's personal work, admirable as it was in terms of charity, was not able within a few years miraculously to transform the instinctive distrust of the Saharan population into open enthusiasm for the French military regime and for the administrative and cultural norms it sought to establish, as if all that was needed was to transplant French civilization and culture—and, which was Charles de Foucauld's concern, Christian ideas and perceptions—by sweeping away the time-honored cultural elements that had shaped the soul of the Muslim people of the Sahara.

Thus, on the one hand, one notes a measure of distrust on the part of the Tuareg, and forms of resistance to what today we would call the cultural aggression of the West, and, on the other hand, a lack of understanding, even in a great mind like Charles de Foucauld. This lack of understanding was heightened by an exclusive attachment to Christian truth and the relativization, if not total reduction, of anything unrelated to the Unique Model, Jesus.

Under these conditions, what did "to tame" really mean? Simply to lead to dialogue, to open-hearted exchanges of views by patient and humble work toward the "establishment of friendship"? Charles de Foucauld exerted admirable efforts in this sense. And this legitimate taming could be rich in possibilities. The Tuareg showed that they were responsive to marks of friendship from their "Christian marabout." They also proved that they were capable of reciprocity. As Muslims, however ill-informed about the Quran, they must have known that in relations between Muslims and authentic Christians, the key word is *friendship*. For it is announced to Muslims in the Quran (V.82) that, among men, Christians will be "the nearest in friendship."

But was this the final stage in "taming" for Charles de Foucauld? Surely not. All his writings and all his missionary activity point to a more profound desire, to prepare the Saharan souls to receive the word of the Gospel. This concern emerges particularly in the correspondence with his friend Henry de Castries: "It is not Evangelization either, in the strict sense of the word. I am neither worthy nor capable of that, and the time has not come. It is the preparatory work for Evangelization, the establishment of confidence, of friendship..." (Letters on June 18, 1904)—an idea that he returns to next month (July 15, 1904) in these words: "My little work goes on...preparatory work.... I have not yet come to sowing. I am preparing the ground, others will sow, others will reap" (LES., p. 130).[14]

But there is a threshold beyond which, it seems to us, he could not reasonably hope to succeed: that is from the moment that the guest and the "Christian marabout" resolved not only to win the hearts of the Tuareg, but their conscience. For it was one thing to seek the friendship of the Muslim population, even to teach them, and to summon them ceaselessly to make them better. It was another thing to try to shatter their certainties in order to induce them to get rid of all, or part, of their beliefs and to give up their ancestral faith. Such a renunciation would have meant the "unraveling" of the intimate fibers of their being.[15]

It was to this very point, in short, that Charles de Foucauld was anxious to lead his Tuareg friends and neighbors gradually. As evidence, there is his attempt to introduce his famous "charity-rosary."[16] An endeavor of this kind could not fail to disturb people instructed in the Muslim religion and to some extent familiar with maraboutic piety. We know that the rosary has an important place in the spiritual exercises instituted by most of the mystical orders in the land of Islam. The number and arrangement of the beads, and the type and order of the prayers ordained to be recited with the rosary, have all been codified from time immemorial by the different maraboutic orders. Each order—even each brotherhood—has as a distinctive sign, certain form of prayer (dhikr), adapted to a certain type of rosary.

In these circumstances, the introduction of a new rosary, even of Islamic inspiration, in a given setting, could be interpreted as a competitive move and a thoroughly hostile gesture. Such an initiative on the part of a Christian—and a foreigner—must have appeared as an unwarranted interference, and consequently unacceptable.

This single rather unwise action of Charles de Foucauld was bound to alienate many sympathies and ruin his "taming" work for good. Instead of "the establishment of friendship," this was the surest way of sowing confusion in people's minds and arousing defensive reactions among his Muslim neighbors. "What is he driving at?" the latter could ask.[17] What is the meaning of his claim to teach Muslims a rosary that is totally foreign to their cultural tradition?

From the moment that doubt enters the mind, questions follow thick and fast. One can then imagine the divergent opinions that the Tuareg could have held about Charles de Foucauld. There was his charitable work, his inexhaustible kindness, his undeniable desire to do good to the Muslims around him. But beyond his silence about the Quran, the Prophet and the saints, as well as on the subject of Muslim practices in general, what were the Christian marabout's innermost feelings about Islam?

# IV

# *The encounter with Islam*

L IKE HIS YOUNG FRIEND LOUIS MASSIGNON (BORN IN
1883), who was in his lifetime an indefatigable Christian
witness for Islam, Charles de Foucauld seems to have
been called by destiny to be a mystical witness to Jesus *before*
Islam.

Louis Massignon was a true witness for Islam, of which he
wished to be the guest and friend and to which he felt doubly
bound in heart and mind: first as a scholar devoted to all the
aspects of truth, and then as a Christian whose fraternal
compassion was in no sense exclusive. He was the great
French Islamicist who gave contemporary Christianity the
first brilliant insight into Islam.

Charles de Foucauld was an impassioned witness for his
Unique Model, haunted by the impatient desire to "bring to
Jesus" the non-Christian population of the colonies. He was
the solitary missionary "long pursued by the thought of the
spiritual dereliction of so many infidels, and in particular of
Muslims..." (ECR. SPIR., p. 260), who never yielded to dis-
couragement in the face of the immensity of the task before
him.

Would this extraordinary vocation have been possible without the first rush of emotion experienced by the young officer
de Foucauld in contact with Islam? It is in the land of Islam,
we know, that Charles de Foucauld felt, if not the irresistible

44

outpouring of grace, at least the initial inner thrill that her-
alded the first movement of his soul toward the paths of faith.
It is a fact that the discovery of the Algerian South was a great
revelation to him.

In this land of light and silence, as if embraced by the
dense, enveloping presence of a sky of unchanging purity,
the young Viscount de Foucauld must have experienced the
most poignant emotions of his life.[1] One can imagine how
deeply moved he was by the spectacle of Muslim prayer in
the open air, as if in direct contact with the supernatural
world, and by the overwhelming intonations of the call of the
muezzin, filling the tranquil immensity of African space with
the eternal words: "*Allāh Akbar,*" words that de Foucauld
would comment on in these terms, in a letter to Henry de
Castries (August 14, 1901): "God is greater, greater than anything we can enumerate" (OEUV.SPIR., p. 622).

Following his reinstatement in the army and return to
Algeria, he was able to rejoin his old friends in the Fourth
Hussars, who had been sent to southern Oran to face the
revolt preached by the marabout Bu Amama (from May
1881). At the end of the eight months that this campaign
lasted, Charles de Foucauld was tempted to prolong his stay
in the South, so impressed was he with the country and its
inhabitants. But when his application for leave was rejected,
he was not able to carry out his plan. Nevertheless, this first
experience of the Algerian South had transformed the man:
"This stay in the south had a happy influence on his destiny:
He came back resolved not only to take life seriously, but
also to achieve something difficult" (GOR., p. 31).

A page had turned in the life of the twenty-three-year-old
Viscount de Foucauld. From now on, he would find himself
almost continually confronted with Islam: on his expedition to
Morocco (1882–1884), on his journey through Algeria and
Tunisia, from Tiaret to Gafsa (September 1885–January 1886);
as a pilgrim in the Holy Land (1888–1889); at La Trappe in

Akbès Syria (1890–1896); in Nazareth and Jerusalem (1897–1900); and finally in the Algerian Sahara (1901–1916).

It is undeniable that the South immediately inspired Charles de Foucauld with an interest in Islam that went beyond a simple curiosity aroused by exotic surroundings. He himself confided to his friend Henry de Castries: "I liked Islam very much, with its simplicity, simplicity of dogma, simplicity of hierarchy, simplicity of morality..." (OEUV.SPIR., p. 622). Whatever Charles de Foucauld's attitude to Islam was to be subsequently—as we shall see later—it is essential to note here the kind of emotions and views that he must have entertained at the beginning of his African experience (both in Morocco and the Algerian South). The exhilarating atmosphere of the desert as well as the mass demonstrations of Muslim piety certainly led the worldly young officer to rediscover, if not the world of prayer, at least that of fervor.

One may well think that Islam had a role not indeed in the blossoming of his spiritual vocation, but in the development of his religious awareness. There have been many opinions about the encounter between the young French officer and Islam. On this subject, the testimony of General Niéger (a great friend of Fr. de Foucauld's) is highly instructive and worth quoting at length: "Should we admit, in private, that Islam influenced Foucauld to the extent of leading him to the brink of conversion? A myth, some say. It is possible, but not proven. And this detail of history will no doubt long remain obscure. As a matter of fact, you rarely meet a man, even a skeptic, among those who have lived for some time on close terms with the Muslims, whose emotions, and some times reason, have not been affected by the outward signs of their simple, profound faith, the spiritual strength given them by an unfaltering religious fatalism, and their religious discipline. The influence of Islam on even the steeliest of characters is all the more powerful when exerted in favorable surroundings, in regions similar to those where it began. It acts by itself, through the setting, and also...geographically, if I can put it that way.

"What is not open to question is that Foucauld's life, on his return from Morocco, was different from the one he had led as a young officer. The long months of moral solitude among Muslims whose acts are deliberately placed under the aegis of the divine will had led him to the idea of the absolute, to religious mysticism. This point can no longer be in doubt today."[2]

Equally enlightening is the opinion of Emile-Félix Gautier, whose acquaintance with Fr. de Foucauld (at Béni-Abbès) goes back to the year 1903.[3] He also admits that "long months of Jewish and Muslim life" so trans- formed the soul of the young Foucauld that he "emerged imbued with Muslim sentiments."[4] He considers this not at all extraordinary for someone who had been in contact with "those religions of the Orient that take possession of the whole soul," and he adds: "When you live among Muslims, you are well aware that Islam has its attrac- tion."[5] But when one has just left the hectic life of the "hyper-civilized" societies of Europe, the attraction of Islam is added to the nostalgia experienced in the pres- ence of the simple life and peace of mind of Muslims. According to E.-F. Gautier, "that feeling nearly led the young explorer to the turban."[6]

Tackling the stage of de Foucauld's conversion under the direction of Abbé Huvelin, E.-F. Gautier, in his inci- sive fashion, takes up the young officer's religious devel- opment after his return from North Africa (1886-1888), as follows: "It was this Abbé Huvelin who effected Fou- cauld's turnabout, and, from a Muslim catechumen, made him a monk 'in five secs.' The friend who told me the story considered, accordingly, that Abbé Huvelin must have been a formidable man."[7]

The learned geographer and historian of North Africa was
not one to be satisfied with "they say" and "approximately."
And so he sought to discover the truth about Charles de
Foucauld and Abbé Huvelin, whom he was determined to go
and see personally ("rue Nollet, Batignolles"). But in vain.
"From neither one," he concedes, "do I have definite confir-
mation of the catechumen's hesitation between the two religions. But the fact was confirmed to me by a reliable source
and is extremely probable; in any case it is not contradicted
by the Father's subsequent attitude."[8]

From all that has been said, one must simply remember
that Islam was at the starting point of Charles de Foucauld's
spiritual journey. Fate would have it that his religious life
and work would develop in constant contact with Islam. But
this relationship would be expressed more in terms of opposition than of open-mindedness and rapprochement.

How can one explain this evolution in de Foucauld's attitude toward Islam, an evolution from the curiosity mixed
with sympathy of his youth, to the lack of understanding,
indeed calm, unwavering rejection of his maturity?

At first sight, psychological factors are not sufficient to
explain this mystery. Conversion, the deepening of Christian
faith, can perfectly well go together with respectful tolerance
of the Islamic faith. We will therefore try rather to understand Charles de Foucauld's attitude to Islam in the light of
socio-cultural factors of the time, taking into account identi-
fiable elements in his knowledge of the Muslim religion and
the Muslim world.

But first, some points of reference. From March 1882 to
June 1883, Charles de Foucauld was in Algiers to prepare for
his great journey to Morocco. He frequented the Bibliothèque
Nationale; he studied Arabic (and Hebrew). After his expedition in Morocco, he spent the summer of 1884 in France
(Paris). From February 1886 to November 1888: a stay in Paris
and trips to the provinces.

Taking into account only these short periods (1882–1883; summer 1884; 1886–1888), during which Charles de Foucauld was able to devote himself to study, it is interesting to consider what might have been the reading of a young man who sought to inform himself about Islam, not as a simple "amateur," but with the desire to acquire an adequate knowledge of the realities and outlook peculiar to a world that he intended to adopt as the field of action and framework for his spiritual life.

It should be noted that, from 1876, the "Nouvelles Asiatiques" of Gobineau (1816–1882) set before a young French generation that was infatuated with exoticism a romantic (and rather disparaging) picture of a conventional Orient of mysterious harems, fabulous caravans, violent passions and fatalism. From "things seen" in Persia, Afghanistan and among the Turkmens, the "Nouvelles Asiatiques" offered an overall view of all levels of society: the nobility, merchants, religious leaders (mullahs and dervishes), and the common people. This was a very attractive introduction to a bookish knowledge of the Orient of that time, which was already no longer a legendary Orient.

For if the vast majority of Muslims continued, as in the past, to live "through imagination and feeling,"[9] certain political officials and the emergent élite sought painfully to adapt themselves to the modern world. It must have been of keen interest for the curious to witness the awakening of modern Islam in a world that was still imbued with medieval ways of thought. And the social structure, occupations and customs of this world constituted an exciting discovery for men conditioned by the scientistic civilization and rationalistic culture of the end of the nineteenth century.

With the advent of the Third Republic and the declaration of colonial policy on the Algerian dominion, many Frenchmen had the opportunity to discover, through Algeria, some of the features of the Orient. Furthermore, with the establishment of the Protectorate in Tunisia (1881), a vast arena of "Oriental" civilization and culture was exposed to French curiosity.[10]

Driven by a taste for exoticism or a desire for adventure (no doubt with the hope of making their fortune), in a colonial domain open to all initiatives, many Frenchmen proved bold enough to cross the Mediterranean. In the wake of soldiers and administrators, traders soon became regular customers of the Marseille-Algiers shipping line. More and more politicians also discovered the African shores, either for the needs of their own personal research or as members of parliamentary commissions of inquiry. The rapid development of trade and relations of all sorts between France and the Algerian-Tunisian region was a chance for many Frenchmen to become aware of the human and cultural problems peculiar to the Muslim societies of North Africa.[11]

Consequently the "Orient" would cease to be a sort of mirage or a purely romantic theme. Stereotypes going back to the "Lettres Persanes" of Montesquieu (1721), and clichés in the style of Gobineau ("Nouvelles Asiatiques," 1876), would fade before concrete knowledge of "oriental" realities. From the Eighties, the news would give an increasingly important place to Muslim affairs (especially through colonial reports). Parallel to the emergence of the Orient—in this case, the Muslim world—in the political and diplomatic sphere, the interest it aroused in scientific circles became more pronounced. Travel books, literary and artistic works inspired by the Orient, university studies of the history, languages and customs of Arab-Muslim societies, all this varied intellectual activity was the sign of an irresistible movement in the West to rediscover the oriental world.

It would have been interesting, in the context of this study, to give a brief survey of the ideas then current about the Orient and the Muslim world, drawing from reports and press comments on colonial and oriental news. This is hardly possible within the confines of a small book. We have recalled above, with the example of Gobineau, the clichés typical of a somewhat superficial literary orientalism. It suf/fices to summarize the dominant images associated with Islam—considered as a cultural heritage, a system of values and a living community—in the European mind toward the end of the last century. We will leave aside popular images that are inevitably unreliable, and to some extent instinctive, to confine ourselves to those that could result from the sci/entific popularization of the century.

In this regard, it is worth considering the teaching of Ernest Renan (1823-1892). As Professor at the Collège de France, Semitic scholar and historian of religions, his opin/ions on Muslim thought and religion were invested with unquestionable authority. His historic essay on "Averröes and Averroïsme" (1855) is famous.[12] Specifically, we will cast our mind back to his lecture on "L'Islamisme et la Science," given at the Sorbonne on March 29, 1883. This important lecture did not go unnoticed. Published the next day (March 30) in "Le Journal des Débats," it gave rise to a famous con/troversy between a Muslim thinker then living in Paris, Jamal al/Dīn al/Afghānī (1839-1897), and the author. Some extracts from this lecture[13] will enable us, on the one hand, to grasp a vision of Islam current in French university circles at the time that concern us, and, on the other hand, to under/stand the strong reactions that Renan's thesis on Islam pro/voked in Muslim élites that were to some extent open to modern ideas of European inspiration.

"Anyone with any knowledge of our time clearly perceives the present inferiority of Muslim countries, the decadence of states governed by Islam, and the intellectual incompetence of races that derive their culture and education exclusively from this religion" (p. 946).

"The liberals who defend Islam do not know it. Islam is the indiscernible union of the spiritual and the temporal. It is the rule of dogma, it is the heaviest fetter that humanity has ever borne" (p. 956).

"Islam has some fine parts as a religion (...), but, as far as human reason is concerned, Islam has been only detrimental (...). It has cut off the countries it conquered from rational intellectual activity" (p. 957).

"In fact, what essentially distinguishes the Muslim is the hatred of science, the conviction that research is useless, trivial, almost impious...(p. 957).

"When one begins with the idea that research is something prejudicial to the rights of God, one inevitably ends with laziness of mind, lack of precision, and the inability to be accurate. *Allah aalam*, 'God knows best,' is the last word in every Muslim discussion" (p. 958).

"Of the two consequences entailed by the lack of scientific spirit, superstition and dogmatism, the second is perhaps worse than the first. The Orient is not superstitious; its great evil is a narrow dogmatism that is imposed by the force of the whole society. The goal of humanity is not repose in resigned ignorance; it is inexorable war against falsehood, the struggle against evil" (pp. 959–960).

Islam, contrary to the scientific spirit; the Islamic faith, incompatible with the rational search for truth; the Muslim mind, incapable of adapting to modernity: these are the main ideas in this lecture. We have here the sort of catalogue of criticisms and negative judgments rarely relinquished by specialists in oriental and Muslim questions at the end of the nineteenth and the beginning of the twentieth centuries.

This vision of Islam was common to many circles (secular and religious) who were concerned, for different reasons, with the Muslim world and the phenomenon of Islam. Politicians and men of letters, including writers of renown,[14] subscribed without qualification to these pessimistic theories. Disparaging opinions of Islam were widely held. The idea of the "intellectual incompetence" of Muslims would be accepted as a fundamental truth. It was customary to pity the fate of the colonial peoples, while at the same time seek- ing to underline their faults, weaknesses and the supposed signs of their decadence.

On the basis of references of a scientific nature, such as the above-mentioned lecture by Renan, some writers were tempted to justify their colonially-inspired political or socio- cultural doctrine: They pronounced on the moral inferiority of the conquered peoples—also designated "degenerate races"—and proclaimed the legitimacy of placing them under European supervision. They even went as far as main- taining the necessity of ridding the people in question of their supposedly "barbaric" culture and traditions, and freeing them—despite themselves—from their religious beliefs, which were regarded as a factor associated with degeneracy and death.

This severity in the historical and moral judgment of Muslims could no doubt be attributed to prejudice and bias. But it is hard to justify the lack of objectivity and composure in the presentation of Islamic questions shown by some Christian writers in the second half of the nineteenth cen- tury, especially when it comes to persons in positions of responsibility.

Take the case of Cardinal Lavigerie, whose teaching and general attitude toward Islam would be regarded by Charles de Foucauld as an example. For this great churchman, this wide-ranging political mind, it seemed that France's trans- Mediterranean mission ought primarily to represent the desire to come to the rescue of "the descendants of the ancient African races, buried for long centuries in the dark- ness of barbarity and death."[15] One notes, by the way, that the words "barbarians" and "barbarity," applied to the Muslims of North Africa, recur in his writings like a leitmotif.[16] In the same way, it is often in terms of darkness and death that the former Archbishop of Algiers refers to the Islamic period in the history of North Africa.[17]

An ardent missionary, Cardinal Lavigerie entertained a view of the Christian apostolate in Africa that led him to minimize the phenomenon of Islam, if not to erase it altogether. Once the conquest and pacification had been completed, he considered that the colonial enterprise should aim to work for the assimilation of the Muslim people "by their free return to civilization and the ancient faith."[18] That is, according to the primate of Africa, "true assimilation, that they seek without ever finding it, *because they seek it with the Quran.*"[19] Hence his conception of an Algeria, and then an African region, gradually integrated into Christianity by the slow work of evangelization and the education of children of Muslim origin, who would come to ask for "baptism themselves one day."[20]

And so to Utopia. But there was no trace of gentleness in the language of the great prelate when he spoke of Muslims—described as "disciples of Mahomet"[21]—and their "sensual religion."[22] This negative attitude toward Islam was to inspire many souls anxious to contribute to the French colonial enterprise, ascribing to it an aim that was moral and spiritual.

\*        \*        \*

We have reviewed some of the French attitudes toward Islam in the last century in order to characterize the moral and intellectual atmosphere in which Charles de Foucauld would have drawn his inspiration and the principles of his future conduct in a Muslim land. It must be admitted that such an atmosphere was hardly conducive to the formation of minds free from all prejudice toward Islam and Muslims. Orientalism concerned itself mainly with the medieval aspects of Muslim thought and civilization, with an erudition that discouraged the non-specialist. Narrative and romantic literature generally delighted in the subjective portrayal of an Orient that was always perceived as a world devoid of values

and creative ideas. Admittedly, French writers of the last cen‑
tury did not go around repeating, after Antiochus:

In the desert of the East, what tedium it was![23]

They found captivating, lyrical tones to celebrate the splendor
of the African landscape and to express their enchantment
with a fairy‑tale world beyond their dreams. But when it came
to speaking of concrete reality, of men in their everyday envi‑
ronment, the same authors changed their tune and even, it
seems, their pen: The enthusiasm of the aesthete then gave
way to the cold reserve of the observer armed with Cartesian
categories and seemingly riveted to cultural and moral norms
held to be absolute.

According to these norms, everything that is not in harmony
with the ethical and cultural models of the Christian West
appears, if not totally devoid of value, at least hardly worthy of
interest. For this reason, studies of the Islamic world most
often dwell on its dark side and deficiencies. What best
engages the attention in sociological analysis or the outward
description of Muslims are features that emphasize medioc‑
rity and popular attitudes that can be attributed to ignorance
and fatalism. In the case of Muslim reactions to foreigners,
those that reveal fanaticism or xenophobia are stressed,
instead of questioning the real motives for these attitudes. In
other parts of the world, they would be regarded simply as
patriotism, opposition to foreigners and the justifiable affir‑
mation of national identity.

In the light of these remarks, it is understandable that his‑
torical observations about Muslim people—and we are
speaking of subject people—tend more toward indictment
than calm, impartial synthesis. The systematic disparage‑
ment of a conquered people leads, in the end, to blaming
them for their own misfortune and "the stubborn determina‑
tion of their decadence."[24] Hence, it is not at all necessary to

justify conquest and colonization with political, economic or strategic arguments. Moral justification for European domi nation would be sought in the present, as in the past, of these people. Thus, far from being presented as the result of acci dents of history and some rather lucky political ventures, French intervention in Algeria would be interpreted instead as the sign of a providential mission.[25]

From these diverse elements, the doctrine of France's civilizing mission was to take shape, a doctrine that would soon enjoy a large consensus in the political community as well as among intellectuals susceptible to this kind of "philosophy of history." Whether under the sign of the Cross, or in the name of republican ideals, the principle of the "moral conquest of the Natives" would appear as the legitimization of military conquest and become the great issue in French colonial circles in the second half of the nineteenth century. Political officials, churchmen and offi cers in the Arab Bureaux would strive to act in accordance with this ideal and to ensure that education, administra tion and all the institutions representing the French pres ence would be "a school for civilization" for the Muslim population of Algeria.

This was the moral and intellectual climate in which French opinion was to be confronted by the colonial problem in general, and the phenomenon of Islam in particular. Charles de Foucauld could not be unaffected by what seemed to be the grand design of his generation, the will to realize, if not the assimilation, at least the social and cultural transformation of the Algerian Muslim people by the double means of French civilization and Christian morality. In the wake of his predecessors and elders, such as Cardinal Lavigerie (1825–1892), the future hermit of Béni-Abbès set his heart on participating, in his way, in the historic mission of his country in the colonial arena.

What for ordinary mortals would be merely a praiseworthy enterprise, motivated by political or humanitarian considerations, assumed for Charles de Foucauld the dimensions of a genuine apostolate, to which he would devote himself with mystical fervor and total self-abnegation.

# V

# Mission accomplished?

THE FIFTEEN YEARS THAT CHARLES DE FOUCAULD SPENT in the Sahara and with the Tuareg of the Hoggar were full years indeed. The great hermit somehow managed to combine the contemplative life with an active life that was exceptionally intense and productive. The numerous biographies of the Universal Brother record this ardent life: of a man of prayer, a scholar and an indefatigable traveler through the boundless desert where he chose to carry out his apostolate.

Charles de Foucauld's scientific work, his social action, his interventions with military officials in the Saharan zone, and all that could be called his temporal work seemed to be a mere extension of his fundamental goal that was spiritual. His many writings and his correspondence give us a good idea of the conception he had of his trans-Mediterranean mission. This mission responded to a double inspiration, one with its source in the Gospel, the other essentially French.

Certainly, his ideal in life, and his constant concern, was the imitation of Jesus. But it is clear that throughout his social and political activities, Charles de Foucauld had an image of France in his mind and an idea of service to France. In his behavior toward the local population (the "Natives"), he saw it as his duty to represent French values. In many different

situations, he strove to act as an officer and a responsible cit-
izen, concerned with the higher interest of his country.

For a missionary of the caliber of Charles de Foucauld,
the image of France was not necessarily identified with that
of a government or an administrative system. His model was
an essentially Christian France, made up of "good priests
and good lay Christians" capable of setting an example of
the evangelical virtues; a France that would furnish the
colonies with good administrators who were altruistic, generous, and able to inspire trust in the Muslims. Charles de
Foucauld fervently hoped that the image of the Frenchman
(the colonial civilian as well as the colonial soldier) would
come to evoke affection for the name Christian and be a
credit to Christianity. Thus Muslims would be led to see
Europeans no longer as "unjust and tyrannical exploiters,
setting an example of vice" (BAZ., p. 409).

Hence the importance he attached to the demand that
officials in charge of Muslim affairs should be worthy to
represent France, politically and morally. Charles de
Foucauld seems to have found the virtues of the leader and
the qualities of the Frenchman embodied in his old friend
Henri Laperrine,[1] commander in chief of the Saharan
Oases (from July 6, 1901), namely: integrity, the gift of sympathy, generosity, nobility allied to simplicity, and respect
for Muslims who he considered ought to be "neither
humiliated nor exploited" (BAZ., p. 236). René Bazin had
good reason to write: "The vocations of Laperrine and de
Foucauld were, then, counterparts...both of a piece, very
French and very Christian" (p. 237).

This former officer, bound in friendship to the military
officials of the Sahara, was tempted to play a part in the
operation that was being carried out virtually before his
eyes: the completion of the conquest and the gradual establishment of French power in the vast area lying between
North Africa and the sub-Saharan zone.[2] In his spiritual

writings and his correspondence, one is aware of his impa-
tience to contribute, in his way, to the pacification of the
newly conquered territories in order to prepare for the
spread of French civilization.

For Charles de Foucauld, the aim of the French presence
in the Sahara—as in North Africa—could not be mere political domination and the static rule of French law over a foreign population that was then entirely left to its own devices.
He believed that this political domination, founded on military conquest, must prepare for the conquest of minds and,
in the very long run, the winning of hearts and the progress
of souls toward the truths of Christianity.

In this light, the role of soldiers, like that of priests and
the laity in general, must be essentially a civilizing role, a
conscious effort to promote the moral and intellectual
progress of the Muslim population. Charles de Foucauld
considered this civilizing work to be of vital importance from
the French as well as from the Christian, point of view.

From the French point of view, the moral and material
progress of the different peoples of North Africa and the
Sahara would not only be a claim to fame but a sort of trump
card for France, who would one day rejoice to find herself
linked to a vast empire, the source of international power and
prestige. In this respect, Charles de Foucauld showed a rare
perspicacity, if one takes into account the accepted ideas of his
age on the colonial question. "If we govern it well," he wrote in
April 1912, "in fifty years' time this empire will be an extension
of France; alas, if we govern it badly, that is if we exploit rather
than civilize, assimilate, and gallicize, this fine empire will
escape from us completely" (TEX.INED., p. 181).[3] A similar
conviction was shared by those ironically termed "Native
lovers" because they showed some sympathy for the "Natives"
and were concerned about their moral and material lot,
instead of viewing the colonial question exclusively from the
point of view of European interests.

Like other liberal and idealistic minds of his generation, Charles de Foucauld identified the colonial enterprise with a mission of human emancipation and civilization. This mission could not be justified in his eyes solely by political arguments for French interests and the grandeur of France. From the Christian point of view, French civilization and culture seemed to him to be essential for the development of morals and attitudes of mind without which specifically missionary activity and the work of evangelization would have no effect on Muslims. This idea would preoccupy Charles de Foucauld throughout his life in the land of Islam. "It is necessary," he wrote to a friend on June 4, 1908, "for the whole country to be covered with monks, nuns, and good Christians remaining in the world to make contact with these poor Muslims, to draw them in gently, to educate and civilize them, and finally, when they are men, to make them Christians. With Muslims, you cannot make them Christians first, and then civilize them; the only possible way is the other, very much slower one: to educate and civilize first, and then to convert later" (ECR.SPIR., p. 238).

These fine resolutions arise from a vision that appears today to be completely Utopian. Nonetheless, Charles de Foucauld did formulate clear instructions on the practical methods to attain this end, which he knew was a remote one, and the "slow and thankless" means to achieve it. The end: the moral and intellectual uplift of Muslims to ensure their "passage to the Gospel." The means, "every means": "to move closer to them, to make contact with them, to strike up friendships with them; through daily, friendly relations, to remove their prejudices against us, and, through conversa⁄ tion and the example of our life, to modify their ideas; to pro⁄ vide instruction, in the strict sense of the word; finally to undertake the complete education of these souls: to teach them, through the schools and colleges, what is learned in schools and colleges; to teach them, by close, daily contact,

what is learned in the family: to become their family ..."
(ECR.SPIR., p. 257).

This is a program of colonial education that goes further
than the most advanced views of the advocates of Franco-
Arab rapprochement and assimilation, to say nothing of the
adversaries of any policy of progress for the Natives, for
whom such a program would appear absurd, and even disas-
trous. Charles de Foucauld, then, held highly personal views
on the subject of colonial policy, and it cannot be said that he
was ever fully in agreement with the military officials or the
colonial administration.

In fact, the military (those "half-Arabs") were, in his
opinion, too respectful of the social status of the population
for whom they had responsibility in the Saharan region,
while at the same time taking no interest in purely cultural
questions. They were generally careful not to undermine
traditional social structures. They relied on the Arab and
Tuareg chiefs, admiring their bravery, political sense and, in
many cases, their panache and amazing prodigality. Charles
de Foucauld himself showed little sympathy for the Arab and
Berber nobles, whom he regarded primarily as the supporters—and beneficiaries—of a feudal system that was incompatible with the new order established by France. Despite
his noble heritage, he had a preference for a "democratic"
policy, conceived in the interest of the common people, the
working classes,[4] rather than the privileged class of nobles
and *ajwād*, that Muslim chivalry who were more in love with
glory than fortune, and for whom the code of honor took the
place of moral and political law.

In contrast to the military officials (and the administrators of the Arab Bureaux), the civil authorities—like Fr. de
Foucauld—had little regard for the "Native chiefs." The
majority of the latter, however, enjoyed real prestige with the
Muslim population. Conscious of being the repositories of a
certain legitimacy (political and religious) and the author-

ized representatives of the Muslim community, the Arab and
Berber nobles had, it seems, a tendency to treat the colonial
bureaucracy with disdain and to consider themselves above
the common law, at least that allegedly embodied by civil
officials of an interfering administration.

The suspicious attitude of French circles in the colony
toward the traditional Muslim nobles soon came to extend
to the rising intellectual élites[5] that aspired to become the
mouthpiece of the Algerian Muslim people, and began to
challenge the methods—and even the legitimacy—of the
colonial system. But this profound distrust of the notables
and the young intellectuals was in no way compensated for
by any concern for the masses. The representatives of the
French colony in Algeria, as well as the administration that
served them, proved unwilling to further the social and
material progress of the Algerian Muslim people and, for
even stronger reasons, their intellectual development.[6]

In these circumstances, the position of Charles de
Foucauld was an uncomfortable one. His ideas on the "native
question" had little in common with colonial realism and consequently could not elicit open support from the custodians of
civil or military authority, and even less from the representatives of the European colony for whom the "Natives" were an
unimportant consideration. The humanism that inspired him
was calculated to alarm the supporters of colonial "orthodoxy" whose objectives were conceived exclusively in relation
to colonization and the European population. His ideal of
brotherhood was incomprehensible to men who were far from
recognizing the human dignity of the Arab or Berber.

Moreover, from the point of view of the political class—in
Algiers as in Paris—who from time to time debated the
native question, the motives that inspired Father de
Foucauld did not have the virtue of agreeing with the ideas
of secular, republican philosophy. His passion for the moral
and intellectual uplift of Muslims was more like that of an

apostle anxious to bring the "infidels" to the spiritual way of Christianity. He advocated with great conviction the neces-sity for the French—officials and ordinary citizens—to cooperate in moral and intellectual progress of Muslims. However, this was not simply for the political satisfaction of seeing France effectively carry out her task of emancipation, but above all to be certain that this moral and intellectual development would so transform people that they would come to "recognize the falsity of their religion and the truth of ours" (ECR.SPIR., p. 256).[7]

Charles de Foucauld's chosen way was unlikely to attract the encouragement of French circles in the colony, with rare exceptions. Nor could it gain him the active sympathy of Muslim circles, in whose eyes the "Christian marabout" appeared primarily in the guise of a Frenchman, and not some lone Frenchman, lost as it were in the Muslim majority, but a Frenchman surrounded, honored and respected by military officials. The ambiguity and the risk of confusion were real, and Charles de Foucauld was aware of it. Hence his fear of seeing Muslims view all Europeans and Frenchmen with the same mistrust: "Will they know how to distinguish between soldiers and priests," he asked, "to see us as servants of God, envoys of peace, universal brothers?" (ECR.SPIR., p. 252).

It was extremely difficult for simple people in the Muslim population of the Sahara to understand the real motives of the Christian hermit. For those who did not have the chance to have frequent contact with him, to know him intimately— as in the case of the Tuareg chief Moussa ag Amastane—the Algerians of the south, like the Tuareg, would wonder in vain about the real mission of this Christian monk and the mean-ing of his presence among them.

Charles de Foucauld's ordinary behavior in his studious, cloistered life, and his lengthy peregrinations,[8] sometimes in the company of military columns, were all rather puzzling to the Saharans. It was a short step to attributing to him some secret political role. In this connection, one must remember his constant dealings with the French military command in the Sahara, either by direct contact or by correspondence.[9] One must note, too, that his concern to set an example of the evangelical virtues went together with a concern to acquaint himself with—and at times even to interfere in—the affairs of the administration and supervision of the Saharan region, as if he felt personally responsible for all that could be accomplished there in the name of France.

Of course, the well informed would see that the "political" activity of the "Christian marabout" could have only beneficial effects. By his very presence, his friendly advice and his exhortations to goodness and justice, he was in a position to exercise a restraining influence on certain military tempers. For this reason, there is no doubt at all that he contributed to mitigating the regime of conquest in force in the "military territories." Although he was concerned with the strengthening of French rule in the whole of northwest Africa, and maintained a keen interest in the pursuit of pacification among the Arab and Tuareg tribes that were not completely subjected to French power, he preached the establishment of a just peace and human relations marked by generosity. Charles de Foucauld rejoiced to see his friend Laperrine exercise a form of government characterized by "a mixture of force employed with justice, unfailing fairness and great gentleness" (LES., p. 126).

But Laperrine was an exceptional case. In a military regime that was based on the search for efficiency, where authority was exercised virtually without control or appeal, there was a great risk that force would be employed indiscriminately or for the sole satisfaction of a will to power. Hence the importance of a voice like Father de Foucauld's, capable of saying no to arbitrary behavior. For instead of remaining quietly aloof from the problems of pacification, the enforcement of order and the organization of the conquest, under the pretext that these temporal affairs lay beyond either his calling or his competence, and instead of remaining silent "like a dumb sentinel," the great hermit behaved like a responsible person,[10] multiplying his appeals and warnings, and suggesting to the representatives of French power a nobler and more exalted objective than immediate domination in the service of a smugly triumphalist policy.

*        *        *

Charles de Foucauld's moderating action in the colonial sphere was not without effect. In addition to Major Laperrine, his old and faithful friend, many of the Saharan officers—like Captains Regnault, De Saint-Léger and Duclos—who were very attached to him, took note of his advice and directives. Thanks to him, a new ethic appeared necessary to govern relations between French officials and the traditional Muslim chiefs. The latter were able to recognize in the behavior of their Christian partners, values that they themselves held sacred: respect for promises, hospitality, and the duty to be honest with adversaries as well as with friends.

This was already the implementation of a policy of dialogue and respect, in happy contrast to the policy of contempt and exclusion that was applied against the "Natives" in the civil territories of the north. It is obvious that from the point of view of French interests, a policy based on justice and respect was more profitable than a policy of force and intimidation. This led Ernest Psichari to say: "I have no idea how many Muslims were converted by the venerable and famous Father de Foucauld in the northern Sahara, but I am certain that he has done more to establish our dominion in that region, than all our administrators, civil and military" (GOR., p. 266).[11]

But despite his virtues and his salutary influence, even despite the fact that he won over to his view several military officials in the Sahara, and important ones at that, the "temporal work of Charles de Foucauld remained an isolated work. This labor of good will and charity unfortunately took place in a harsh context. The colonial process offered few opportunities for the full development of a liberating humanism in the spirit of the Gospel. The attitudes of mind were not there to promote a fruitful rapprochement between communities and cultures.

In fact, the empire taking shape on the other side of the Mediterranean was still insecure and seemed to require the mobilization of all energies to consolidate French ascendancy. It was not the time for sentimental outbursts and humanitarian observations on the fate of the local population. Algeria and its Saharan extension was the scene of a mighty confrontation between two types of mentality, civilization and cultural tradition. An historic drama on this scale gave rise to too much human passion for the voice of charity and brotherhood to have a decisive influence at that time.

On the one side, there was a community of Muslims, proud of their past and jealous of their independence, who found it hard to submit to a nation that was totally foreign to them in language, religion and customs. On the other side, there was an armed force carried away by the dynamic of victory, elated with the feeling of being in the vanguard of the builders of a modern empire. There was, too, an effectively organized European colony, endowed with all the means of economic prosperity and resolved to manage the diverse resources of an immense region for its own profit, regardless of the legitimate aspirations of the "Natives."

Against the background of these political (and religious) forces, what could be the significance of the personal effort of a man reduced—as Charles de Foucauld was—to the sole resources of charity and prayer? Amid tensions engendered by the clash of cultures, the antagonism of races and the unleashing of material desires, what good was this solitary voice, whose echoes seemed to come from the end of the world?

It is true that at the local level, Charles de Foucauld's benevolent action was able to have immediate effects. It would take a long time to enumerate his services to the Saharan and Tuareg peoples as well as to his French military friends: thanks to him, many afflictions were relieved, wrongs put to right, blunders made good and needless tragedies averted in the nick of time. But the saintly hermit's action could not—by some miracle—decisively alter the course of history. The colonial process, apparently irreversible, pursued its logical development: the gradual reduction of the native element in the social and economic spheres; increasingly severe restrictions on the freedoms of Muslim subjects (freedom of assembly and travel, freedom of access to economic activities and to positions in traditional teaching, etc.).

In a situation where the stakes were so high, since the very future of the French presence in Africa was in question, men of God (like prophets and poets!) had no say in the matter. Although Charles de Foucauld's temporal work was in harmony with the broad line of official policy, it was too modest, and doubtless too idealistic, to be considered a decisive contribution to his country's colonial enterprise.

After all, by its very nature, Charles de Foucauld's "policy" was not likely to achieve successes comparable to those of the policy practiced by the military and civil officials in the colony. They did not refer to the same norms, and did not aim at the same objective in the field of either culture or civilization.

Despite its fortunate moral and social effects—that are indicated above—Charles de Foucauld's temporal activity in reality had little chance of lasting fulfillment. For this activity took place in an atmosphere charged with grave psychological and moral tensions arising from the racial and cultural confrontation. Under these circumstances, while recognizing the nobility of his motives and the generosity of his views, it is fair to point out the limitations and failures of Charles de Foucauld's efforts in pursuit of his political design.

The uprisings against French authority in the Sahara during the years of the First World War, and the tragic episode at Tamanrasset (December 1, 1916) that cost the great missionary his life,[12] all lead one to think that the best part of Charles de Foucauld's work in the Sahara was not that devoted to the support of his country's policy. And it is certainly not the image of the "Colonizer-monk" (BAZ., p. 320) that will be remembered in the end.

\*        \*        \*

One can then, from the Muslim point of view, reflect upon Charles de Foucauld's mission and the ultimate significance of his testimony before Islam. Referring to the example of Christ, the great hermit noted: "St. John cites our Lord's last words to His Father: 'I have accomplished all that you gave me to do.' My God, may these words be ours, in our last hour! Not in the same sense, with the same perfection: We are miserable mortals, but insofar as is possible in our wretchedness" (ECR.SPIR., p. 35).[13]

What is left of this mission accomplished by the Little Brother of Jesus? And, from the Islamic point of view, what is the message that endures?

# Conclusion:
# The strait way

CHARLES DE FOUCAULD'S SAHARAN LIFE represents an existence centered on an ideal of holiness that was reflected in renunciation and the humble imitation of Jesus. Far from the attractions of the world, far even from the ordinary means of charity, he chose the *Strait Way*, to walk in the steps of his divine Master: "If anyone wishes to follow me, let him deny himself daily and follow me" (ECR.SPIR., p. 165—cf. Luke 9:23; Matthew 16:24; Mark 8:34).

His life of renunciation and silence, with a fondness for "that dear lowest place" of the simple "workman son of Mary" (ECR.SPIR., p. 189), was nonetheless an intensely active life and a deeply felt presence in his place and time, through his everyday activities, his intellectual work and his extensive correspondence. For a man like Charles de Foucauld could not become totally absorbed in a strictly contemplative life. He was driven by a desire to teach— admittedly, more by example than by word—and to make the Truth shine forth, the Truth that stirred him to the core of his being. He aspired with a restrained but unremitting passion to open, in what he regarded as a moral desert, a new way to Jesus. He expended all his energy and fervor to make this way radiant and somehow irresistible.

Truth and Way are words that often recur in Charles de Foucauld's "Ecrits Spirituels." Muslim saints have also preached their Truth and their Way, recognizing that divine Truth is one, although the ways that lead there are different, as are the prophetic messages and other signs that make it perceptible to men. In fact, Islam does not have a "horror" of diversity. Within the faith, the normative pluralism in matters of religious law is regarded as a "divine grace." Outside Islam, denominational pluralism is accepted in the spirit of tolerance that reinforces the special respect granted by the Quranic revelation to the People of the Book (Jews and Christians). "To each of you," proclaims the Quran, "we have appointed a right way and an open road. If God had willed, He would have made you one nation; but that He may try you in what has come to you. So be you forward in good works; unto God shall you all return" (V, 48).

Consequently, the testimony of someone like Charles de Foucauld in the land of Islam ought in no way to constitute an offense for a Muslim. In the case of a man who exerted all his moral strength to live in devotion to Christ, how could one not recognize the signs of those *naṣārā* whom the Quran cites as an example: "Those who say: 'We are Christians'" (see the beautiful verse V, 82, already quoted); that is, those with whom the Book recommends us "to dispute in the better way," and to whom it is right to say: "We believe in what has been sent down to us, and what has been sent down to you; our God and your God is One, and to Him we have surrendered" (XXIX, 46).

Far be it from us, however, to draw a veil over all that, in Charles de Foucauld's missionary zeal, was likely to hurt Muslim feelings. We have drawn attention above to the stereotypes about Islam conveyed by the culture of the time, stereotypes that the great hermit often repeated without discrimination. We have noted how illusory it was to hope to convert the Muslim population of the Sahara, who in his eyes were "slaves of error and vice" (ECR. SPIR., p. 260), and whom he wished to rescue from their "spiritual dereliction." Although he was prompted by a charitable sentiment to cooperate in the salvation of men whom he regarded as brothers, his distressing train of thought (some would say obsession) when he contemplated the moral and religious state of the Muslims of North Africa appears to have been profoundly affected by a vision of the world peculiar to the Christian culture of his time.

Moreover, from a strictly Algerian point of view, it may appear justifiable to consider Father de Foucauld's attitude in critical terms. There are good grounds for this: on the one hand, there are the political views of the former officer, who remained to the end a supporter of French expansionism in Africa; on the other hand, there is his actual solidarity with the colonial regime, the true nature of which had doubtless escaped him. Furthermore, he was not able to perceive all the repercussions of colonialism on Algerian Muslim opinion, from which he was virtually cut off in his remote solitude.

In spite of everything, it seems to us unjust to blame a monk like Charles de Foucauld for not being able to transcend the outlook of his time, and reveal to the world political truths that the Algerians and the French would take almost half a century to recognize. If he was not, in this sphere, what would call a genius as a forecaster, he was nonetheless more clear-sighted than most of the colonial officials of his generation, and did not hesitate to warn his compatriots that they would lose their African empire for lack of a policy of justice and progress and a genuine desire to emancipate the native population.

The truth demands that Charles de Foucauld be considered in a context that was truly his own: not that of an officer, a colonial administrator or an ideologue, but purely in a spiritual context. In this context, de Foucauld has left his mark as an exemplary figure. The famous "Christian

marabout," it seems to us, completed an irreplaceable testimony before the Muslim community as he sought to bring
evangelical charity and spirituality to life. He strove to
embrace all the virtues that were identified with Christians
in the Quranic revelation, setting an example of active
brotherly love, humility and inexhaustible gentleness.
Despite the difficult historical conditions and the tempta-
tions to injustice or intolerance that lay in wait, not only for
those responsible for French policy in the Maghrib, but for
every Christian implicated in the colonial process, he sought
the friendship of Muslims and attempted to establish a way
of living together as brothers.

Furthermore, he proved that this desire for brotherhood
was not a kind of platonic or intellectual aspiration. Living
among the Tuareg, he shared their lot, seeing them not as
strangers but as neighbors, friends and brothers. His dedication to the Tuareg people and to the country of his adoption would endure until his death.

Out of devotion to the African land to which he had given
his best, Charles de Foucauld made a vow to "rest there
until the resurrection." And this was indeed his fate. Under
the circumstances, would it be too much to think that,
although he may belong to Christianity spiritually, the great
hermit of the Sahara belongs in some way to Islam, since he
chose a Muslim country for his last dwelling place?

The Muslim honors this exceptional figure: A man who
calmly embraced the rejection of all earthly joys and tried at
all times to act "only seeking the good pleasure of God"
(Quran, LVII, 27).

All this did not escape his great friend the Tuareg chief,
Moussa ag Amastane, who grieved for him sincerely, and
whose letter to Madame de Blic expresses profound sorrow:
"When I heard of the death of our friend, your brother
Charles, my eyes closed; everything turned dark; I wept and
shed many tears, and I am in deep mourning" (BAZ., p. 466).

These words need no comment, for a man like the Tuareg chief was incapable of sentimentality, and he had no need to feign such grief.

The truth is that Moussa Ag Amastane and his co-religionists were in a position to recognize Charles de Foucauld as something other than a passing guest or an obliging friend—a foreigner. From his words and deeds and his enduring concern to share their difficult material conditions, they must have understood that he wished—and felt himself—to be with them simply as a man with his brothers.

\*       \*       \*

In view of so many sacrifices and so many efforts at fraternal rapprochement, even if it was part of a plan to "tame" others in order to unite them to the family of Christ, must we refuse to forgive Charles de Foucauld for a style of apostolate that was marked by a simplistic conception of the moral and religious values of others? The man did not claim to be infallible. Neither did he claim to act in the name of some brand of modern humanism, mindful only of earthly values. This was a profoundly Christian soul, a mystical soul, who saw the absolute only in Jesus. Who would presume to cast a stone at a man who consecrated his entire life to this absolute?

Beyond the inevitable blunders and errors of judgment (of which Charles de Foucauld was probably unaware), there remains this exceptional human adventure that will continue to summon the Muslim as well as the Christian consciousness. And we will long ponder on the mysterious impulse that led this son of Alsace to the Sahara and then to the heart of Ahaggar (Hoggar), where he tried to humanize a country so wild that it seemed to be torn from a lunar world.

Because he decided one day to plant his hermitage there (May 1910), facing the tortured landscape of Ahaggar, the promontory of Assekrem became one of those sacred places where the spirit lives and breathes. Imprinted there forever,

Charles de Foucauld's image has become a source of radi-
ance in the solitude and silence. It reminds us of the
"monk's lamp" dear to the ancient Arab poets, with its glim-
mer that made the heart of the solitary traveler beat with
gladness, at the thought that through the unfathomable
desert night, this fragile light was like the joyful sign of a fraternal presence.

# Abbreviations

In the text, we quote on a number of occasions, in an abridged form, the following references:

BAZ.        = René Bazin, *Charles de Foucauld—*
              *Explorateur du Maroc—Ermite au*
              *Sahara*, Paris, Plon, 1921.

ECR.SPIR.   = *Ecrits Spirituels de Charles de Fou-*
              *cauld—Ermite au Sahara—Apôtre*
              *des Touaregs*, Paris, J. De Gigord, 12th
              ed., 1951.

GOR.        = Georges Gorrée, *Sur les Traces de*
              *Charles de Foucauld*, Paris–Lyon, 2nd
              ed., 1936.

LES.        = Paul Lesourd, *la Vraie Figure du Père*
              *de Foucauld*, Paris, Flammarion,
              1933.

NIE.        = General Niéger, "Laperrine et le Père
              de Foucauld vus par un Saharien," in
              *Construire*, ed. J. Dumoulin, Paris
              XIII, 1943, pp. 179–205.

OEUV.SPIR.　　=　*Oeuvres Spirituelles*

POES.TOUAR.　=　*Poésies Touarègues—Dialecte de l'Ahaggar—Recueillies par le P. de Foucauld*, work publised by André Basset, Paris, E. Leroux, vol. 1, 1925; vol. 2, 1930.

SIX.　　　　　=　Jean-François Six, *Itinéraire Spirituel de Charles de Foucauld*, Paris, ed. Seuil, 1958.

TEX.INED.　　=　Charles de Foucauld, *Contemplation— Textes inédits*, ed. Beauchesne, Paris, 1969, 189 p.

# Translator's Afterword

## Merad's Response to Charles de Foucauld

IN HIS PREFACE, MERAD SETS OUT THE REASONS for producing "yet another book" to add to the plethora of works that pay tribute to Charles de Foucauld. He observes that among the many Christian studies, there is nothing by a Muslim. Conscious of an "undefinable void," he offers an Islamic view of "this Christian life implanted in the heart of an Islamic land."

On a more personal note, Merad emphasizes that his book does not claim to provide "*the* Islamic answer" to the "case" of Charles de Foucauld. Nor is it an academic exercise, motivated by purely intellectual curiosity. It is simply an attempt to make sense of his own experience that he describes as "a living summons."

Exploring the nature of this summons, Merad points to the powerful attraction of holiness that transcends historical contingency and the diversity of culture and belief. Charles de Foucauld spoke "to Christians and to Muslims in the language of the Gospel," through his life lived in imitation of Jesus.

This imitation of Jesus is the central theme of Merad's book. He perceives principles that accord with "the Qur'anic revelation and the pure tradition of primitive Islam," and this perception lies at the heart of his contribution to the Christian-Muslim dialogue. It is also the driving force behind his own interpretation of the role of Charles de Foucauld.

At the beginning of his inquiry, Merad recognizes that "it is urgent to surmount the age-old barriers, maintained by mistrust and prejudice, and weighed down with grievances accumulated in the course of a long historical process marked by relations of force and domination." It is, therefore, important to avoid the language of confrontation.

Furthermore, as an historian, Merad warns against the tendency to read back into the past the concerns of the present and to expect great men to hold views that belong to a later age. Charles de Foucauld was shaped by his education, his military training and the ethos of colonialism. His mind was conditioned by the prevalent opinions, imagery and unconscious assumptions of his class. Merad depicts him as very much a man of his day. This interpretation necessitates a careful review of the historical and cultural background of the Frenchman's attitude to Islam.

The moral and intellectual climate of late nineteenth century Europe was characterized by a distinctive set of ideas. Infected by the mania for classification rife at the time, the French aristocrat Gobineau, in his *Essay on the Inequality of Human Races* (1853–1855), advanced a theory that divided mankind into pure and degenerate races. Renan (d. 1892), the philosopher and orientalist, in a famous lecture entitled *Islam and Science,* described Islam as intellectually inferior, incompatible with science, and incapable of adapting to the modern world. Lavigerie (d. 1892), the Archbishop of Algiers and founder of the White Fathers, held similar unliberal views. He commonly referred to the Muslims of North Africa as barbarians and described the Islamic period in terms of darkness and death.

At the same time, Gobineau produced the *Nouvelles Asiatiques* that pictured an Orient of mysterious harems, fabulous caravans and grand passions. A young Romantic was led to project his own emotions onto remote times and places to create what has been called "a country of his own imagining."[1]

Popular writers, Merad charges, were enchanted with the fairy-tale world of Africa, "but when it came to speaking of concrete reality, of men in their everyday environment, the same authors changed their tune...the enthusiasm of the aes-thete then gave way to the cold reserve of the observer armed with Cartesian categories, and seemingly riveted to cultural and moral norms held to be absolute." The Muslim world was judged by the standards of the West and found wanting.

A whole system of knowledge about the Orient underlies Charles de Foucauld's outlook and, Merad claims, accounts for the change in his attitude to Islam, "from the curiosity mixed with sympathy of his youth, to the lack of understand-ing, indeed calm, unwavering rejection of his maturity." Merad possibly underestimates the psychological mechanism that can cause a person to react against previously strong feel-ings of attraction. However, he is undoubtedly correct to emphasize the influence of the prevailing stereotypes about Islam that the great hermit tended to repeat indiscriminately.

In his analysis of these stereotypes and their association with colonialism, Merad anticipates the argument so force-fully advanced several years later by Edward Said in *Orientalism*. Like Said, Merad too links popular racial theo-ries with colonialism, showing how the "systematic dispar-agement of a conquered people" provided a justification for European domination. The idea of backward or subject races served to legitimize the "moral conquest of the natives" and to reinforce France's civilizing mission.

An ardent patriot, Foucauld wholeheartedly endorsed his country's expansionist ideals. Dedication to the service of France ran like a leitmotif through his life, from his early career as a soldier and his work as an explorer (with its polit-ical and military implications), to his collaboration with the army in the Sahara, both as an interpreter and as a source of military intelligence. His criterion for any action was always whether it would be favorable to the prosperity and power of France. Bazin describes him as "one of the greatest propa﹣gators of French influence in the Sahara."[2]

Although a supporter of the colonial system and the French presence in North Africa, Charles de Foucauld shared the enlightened views of his friend Colonel (later General) Laperrine, the great military commander of the desert who was known to tribesmen as "the man with a white heart." Both men saw the need to be sensitive to the feelings of the local populace. They stressed the importance of fairness and respect, and held that Muslims should be neither humiliated nor exploited. The hope was that the indigenous peoples would come to love, and therefore to imitate, their conquerors. Ultimately North Africa would be re﹣created in the image of France—for Foucauld, a very Christian France, "the France of Charlemagne, St. Louis and Joan of Arc."[3]

In fact, the civilizing mission was bound up with conver﹣sion. The aim of its protagonists was "to colonize the African territory of the mother country, not to enrich them﹣selves, but to make France loved, to make French souls and, above all, to procure their eternal salvation!"[4] The method, according to Charles de Foucauld, was "to edu﹣cate and civilize first, and then to convert later." This objective he shared with Lavigerie, although Foucauld was the more realistic, admitting that it might take a century to attain! Both men fully identified with the grand design of their generation, "to realize, if not the assimilation, at least the social and cultural transformation of the Algerian Muslim people, by the double means of French civilization and Christian morality." Not surprisingly, evangelization has been described as one of the most important arms of colonialism."[5]

It is easy to criticize such views in the light of contemporary criteria. However, it must be remembered that, as Said points out, a hundred years ago every European was "a racist, an imperialist, and almost totally ethnocentric."[6] Seen in this context, one has to appreciate Merad's balanced and fair assessment of the achievement of Charles de Foucauld.

On the positive side, Merad shows how Foucauld's views on colonial policy differed from those of both the colonial administration and the army. With reference to the native population, Foucauld deplored that "we know them so little" and "we do nothing for them," and warned that if the French persisted in their greed, violence and disregard for the welfare of the people, in the end "we will lose everything, and the union that we have made of this people will turn against us."[7] He even predicted the rise of nationalist movements led by an intellectual elite that would use Islam "as a lever to stir up the ignorant masses, and will seek to create an independent Muslim African empire."[8]

Merad accepts that Charles de Foucauld, with his exhortations to justice and mercy, exercised a restraining influence on the military regime, and helped to introduce a new ethic into relations between French officials and the traditional Muslim chiefs. On a personal level, there were his "little, nameless, unremembered acts of kindness and of love."[9]

However, as Merad observes, this labor of good will took place in an adverse setting, "amid tensions engendered by the clash of cultures, the antagonism of races and the unleashing of material desires." Charles de Foucauld's was a lonely voice and an ambiguous one. His devotion to the army and to the ideal of French supremacy never wavered. His association with the forces of occupation was close, and everyone knew of it. He himself was well aware of the difficulties of his position and wondered: "Will they know how to distinguish between soldiers and priests, to see us as servants of God, envoys of peace, universal brothers?"

The influence of the ideas of the time—the widespread belief in Western superiority and the "subject races"—is manifest in Foucauld's writings and actions. The word "taming," adopted by both Foucauld and Laperrine, reflects what Said calls the myth of arrested development and the "rescue theme." The Muslim peoples of the Sahara were to be liberated from their "spiritual dereliction" and delivered to Western religion and culture.

There is a strong flavor of paternalism in the Christian marabouts's relations with the Tuareg chief Mousssa ag Amastane. Despite the real admiration and respect on both sides, Foucauld had serious misgivings about his friend, particularly when the latter's influence increased and he showed a penchant for independent action. Charles de Foucauld preferred to "envelop him in paternal solicitude." Their complex relationship is described with considerable insight and sensitivity by Merad, who provides a valuable insider's view to counter the usual idealized version. He discerns a lack of warmth and depth in the friendship. The whole account illustrates the "irreducible distance"[10] inherent in a relationship based on power, a distance that makes genuine comradeship impossible.

Merad concludes that although Charles de Foucauld's motives were good, he shared the prejudices of his time and became enmeshed in worldly affairs for which he was peculiarly unsuited. He made a series of errors of judgment and his positive contribution was too modest to make a substantial difference. What, then, did he achieve?

To answer this question, it is necessary to look beyond the inevitable shortcomings of Foucauld's age and background to his avowed purpose in life: to imitate Jesus. Merad maintains that a "perfect imitation of Jesus by a Christian must assume a great moral and spiritual significance in the eyes of Muslims."

He at once compares the imitation of Jesus to the imitation of the Prophet, the true sign of faith for a Muslim. In the Qur'an, the faithful are called upon to regard the Prophet as a "good example" (Q.33:21), and Muslims respond by imitating him in both a literal and an ethical sense. It is because of his own experience of personal discipleship that Merad can spontaneously empathize with the imitation of Jesus.

What does the Christian imitation of Jesus mean to a Muslim? Merad stresses that the primary source for the Islamic understanding of Christianity is the Qur'an, and it is there that one must look for Muslim expectations of Christians.[11] A number of positive statements can be found. Merad cites the well-known passages that ascribe to Christians "kindness and mercy" (Q.57:27), and note their absence of pride (Q.5:82). Christians are also described as the "nearest in friendship" to Muslims (Q.5:82), a phrase that has become a key text for the Christian-Muslim dialogue.[12]

In the Islamic tradition, Jesus is associated above all with poverty and unworldliness.[13] This image is reflected in sayings attributed to him, especially by the early Sufis for whom he represented the ideal ascetic. Al-Ghazali quotes a tradition that Jesus said: "I go to sleep, possess nothing, and I rise in the morning, possess nothing, and there is none upon earth who is richer than I."[14] Even simple people in the Muslim world know that Jesus "went barefoot" and "had nowhere to lay his head."

The Christian monk (rāhib) was regarded as a "friend of Jesus" and respected as a remnant of his original community, referred to as a "community apart." The Qur'an praises the humility of priests and monks and commends their practice of mortification. According to al-Ghazali, the four things that guard against "bandits" on the road to God are solitude, silence, fasting and vigils.[15] Although monasticism is condemned, it is accepted that the motive is to please God and there is evidence that a genuine sympathy existed between Muslims and monks in the early days.[16]

The whole notion of self-renunciation, so near the core of Christian ethics, has a powerful appeal to Muslims. Merad remarks that they are particularly impressed by the sacrifice of Europeans who give up the good things of this world to share the lot of the poor in the deserts and mountains of an alien land. The sense of wonder is evident in the Tuareg chief's letter to Charles de Foucauld on the former's return from France. He tells how he visited the hermit's family and saw their fine homes and gardens, and ends: "And there you are in Tamamrasset, like a pauper." Merad concludes that, from the Muslim point of view, the imitation of Jesus responds to the Islamic expectation of the People of the Book, and is "the most eloquent way to espouse the authenticity of the Gospel message."

This Christian idea of holiness is in marked contrast to the cult of saints, or maraboutism, that is the hallmark of Islam in North Africa.[17] At the time of Charles de Foucauld, marabouts,[18] rural holy men who must be distinguished from genuine Sufi mystics, exerted immense influence in the Sahara. In addition to officiating at devotions, festivals and pilgrimages, they presided at functions such as marriages, dispensed justice, and controlled instruction through their Qur'an schools. The sheikh exercised almost unlimited authority over his followers: A disciple was bound to his master by an oath of allegiance and was expected to be "like a corpse in the hands of the washer." In the wrong hands, this attitude of utter subservience could lead to "a refined form of spiritual tyranny."[19]

Exploitation was widespread. Marabouts, especially the shurfa, those who claimed descent from the Prophet, enjoyed a range of economic rights over the faithful. Gifts coupled with tithes provided the marabouts with a lucrative livelihood, enabling them to live as "glorious parasites."[20]

The ascendancy of the marabouts was enhanced by a belief in their magical powers, manifested in miracles (karāmāt) and terrifying curses that entailed threats of sudden death, disease or disaster. The resultant aura of mystery helped the marabout to maintain a deliberate distance from the run of his followers. He was believed to have the power of intercession and to possess *baraka*, a mysterious supernatural force found in certain persons and things and passed down from father to son.

Thus the *walī*, or friend of God, inspired fear and superstitious respect. As Gellner neatly puts it, there was "a flow of goods and services upward compensating for the spiritual flow downward."[21] Merad writes of the marabouts' unique position: "Since they were spiritual masters, patrons and nobles all at the same time, the entire community of the faithful was theoretically subject to them."

One can appreciate how mystified the Tuareg must have been by their Christian marabout who sought to imitate "the hidden life of the poor, humble workman of Nazareth." From the time of his first visit to the Holy Land, Charles de Foucauld had adopted Nazareth as his model. Throughout his life, he strove to reproduce Jesus' obscurity, silence and humility (expressed in what he called "littleness" and his concept of the "lowest place"), and joyfully embraced "manual work and holy poverty." He came to identify Tamanrasset with Nazareth and lived there among the people without ceremony, mystery or any claim to unusual powers.

Unlike the marabouts, for whom all the faithful were servants, Charles de Foucauld assumed the vocation of Servant Marabout and, following Jesus, devoted himself to a life of loving service. He endeavored to treat each person as "not a man, but Jesus," and gave to everyone in need: food to the hungry, remedies to the sick and comfort to the troubled. He deliberately sought out the most menial tasks, washing and cleaning for the poor, in order "to be like Jesus, who was among the apostles as 'the one who serves.'"

Above all, he gave the gift of himself. He was constantly available and, as he said, "knowing that I am always here, people come to see me." Despite continual interruptions of his work and prayer, he kept no one waiting. The spare figure at the door, with the welcoming smile and outstretched hand, offered a resting place to travelers, knitting lessons to women, and little gifts and jokes to the children who adored him. With his respectful attentiveness to their needs, the Christian marabout treated the poor nomads not as cases, but as well-loved brothers. His program of "love, love, kindness, kindness" won the confidence and gratitude of the Tuareg, who would later pray at his tomb: "May God raise the marabout high in Paradise, for he was good to us in this life."

The practice of prayer and charity did not prevent him from assuming the prophet's role of speaking out against injustice. Merad quotes with approval Foucauld's statement: "We must not interfere in the secular government ...but we must 'love justice and hate iniquity,' and when the secular government commits a great injustice...we do not have the right to be 'sleeping sentinels,' 'silent watchdogs,' 'uncaring shepherds.'"

Charles de Foucauld did not hesitate to denounce the French treatment of Algerians, criticize excesses of the army and, most of all, campaign against slavery, "this huge and monstrous injustice" that flourished in the Sahara with the permission of the French government. Beyond condemning the practice as immoral and unjust, he offered slaves food and shelter, and bought and liberated some of them himself.

Merad sees a parallel between Charles de Foucauld's involvement in the issues of the day and the Islamic obligation, the Call to Good. This injunction derives from the Qur'anic command to enjoin good and forbid evil (Q.3:104), and is a fundamental principle of Islamic ethics. Merad perceives that in following Jesus, Charles de Foucauld was a true Christian. At the same time, with his total submission to God, his moral achievement and his endeavor to build a better world, the hermit was living in the spirit of pure Islam.

Charles de Foucauld was a man "consumed by an inner fire that was, for him, the love of Jesus." He believed that a natural effect of love was imitation, and for one who sought to love like Jesus, the love of God and neighbor not only went together but were, in fact, one and the same. This love found expresion in his "care over lives of humble people,"[22] and earned the regard of his Muslim neighbors, who knew him as the Marabout Abed Aissa (servant of Jesus).

It was the holiness of the Christian hermit's life that "sum-moned" Merad and inspired him to record his own reaction. Reflecting, as a Muslim, on the meaning of Charles de Foucauld's witness in the desert, Merad is driven to ask: "Under the circumstances, would it be too much to think that, although he may belong to Christianity spiritually, the great hermit of the Sahara belongs in some way to Islam?"

## Some Lessons for the Christian-Muslim Dialogue

What can be learned from this Islamic response to the example of Charles de Foucauld? What are the lessons for the Christian-Muslim dialogue? Panikkar has proposed some Rules of the Game for the religious encounter.[1] In a situation that is less clear-cut than a game, the term convention[2] may be preferable. For human relations are not governed by explicit rules so much as by a pattern of subtle signals that embody expectations and impose limits on our behavior.

What follows is an effort to set out some conventions for the guest. The word is used by Merad, and also by Charles de Foucauld and his friend, the French Islamicist Louis Massignon (d. 1962), who wrote: "To understand the other, one does not need to annex him but to become his guest."[3] To what extent do we try to annex Muslims rather than to act as guests in the House of Islam?

The Oxford English dictionary defines a guest as one who is entertained at the house of another, that is, an outsider temporarily admitted inside. The guest is physically not at home. Yet conferences on Islam, in the most cases in the West initiated by Christians, are often held in seminaries or on church premises, where the would-be guests are at home, but the hosts are not. One must not underestimate the effect of the setting on Muslims, who are usually greatly outnum-bered on these occasions, and of the whole atmosphere of the meeting, which is seldom on their own ground.

This consideration has added importance if the ground is interpreted more broadly to include the agenda of the meet-ing, generally drawn up by Christians. The procedure may be scrupulously fair: suggestions are invited and equal time is allotted to each side. Nevertheless, non-Muslims set the agenda, and the assumptions, expectations and objectives reflect contemporary Western thinking.

For example, in an attempt to define the "dialogic men-tality," some have proposed preconditions that would exclude anyone with a claim to have "the final word" or the "definitive revelation." Swidler decrees that "only those who have a deabsolutized understanding of truth will in fact be able to enter into dialogue."[4] Such a proviso rules out not only the vast majority of Muslims but a number of Chris-tians as well, and may account for the restricted and unrep-resentative nature of may of the groups that do meet. Knitter is tempted to confront objectors with "the question of how they can really play the game of dialogue when they have been given all the trump cards by God."[5] One could surely ask who lays down the rules and whose game it is anyway.

In the contemporary dialogue, there is great emphasis on the necessity for openness, which is linked to the prospect of change and transformation.[6] However, while the statement "I want to be changed" is invariably greeted with applause in the West, it is not received with wholehearted enthusiasm elsewhere. For the many who do not equate growth with mere change (with its overtones of innovation), and who believe that there can be no growth without continuity, the openness of dialogue appears less as an exciting spiritual adventure than an undesirable leap in the dark. Knitter compares dialogue without the possibility of transformation to "a sleek aircraft that can take us anywhere but is not allowed to land."[7] He does not consider that many may not choose to board such a plane in the first place, bound for an unknown destination. Moreover, when the call for change is associated with an assertion of the truth of Christianity, it begins to sound dangerously like conversion. This impression augments the suspicion of sinister motives behind the conferences on Islam.

We are often unable to see how much we are imposing our way of thought on others in a manner that assures our advantage. The form the dialogue takes under such conditions is felt by many Muslims to be both uncongenial and irrelevant. Nasr has asked: "Why are Christians much more interested in dialogue than Muslims?" and he goes on to charge the West with developing a model that does not correspond to any reality on the Islamic side.[8]

What conventions, then, can help to shape and sustain the special relationship of partners in dialogue? What are the qualities that distinguish the good guest in the House of Islam?

In the first place, there must be a certain deference to the principles and practices of the house. The good guest recognizes that there are boundaries to his role and exercises restraint. He need not always agree with his host, but he does not confront him with supposed deficiencies in his own home. A good guest does not move the furniture.

For example, it is unacceptable for non-Muslims to insist on discussing the Qur'an in terms of sources, influences and historical reliability. During a debate at Harvard, when Hans Küng called for the application of the methods of modern critical scholarship to the Qur'an,[9] Nasr replied that this was sheer blasphemy in the eyes of a Muslim. In fact, any insensitive affront to religious sensibilities is not only wounding but counter-productive. It tends to evoke the traditional reaction from Muslims, which is to avoid the arguments of unbelievers (Q.28:55).[10] Muslims may appear to refuse to hear, but to hear, you have to listen, and you cannot listen if you have to turn away.

Merad proves to be the ideal guest in his observance of the conventions of courtesy and tact. He recognizes that his treatment of Charles de Foucauld may appear presumptuous and acknowledges the limitations of an outsider, who by definition lacks "that inner knowledge, sustained by religious feeling and the communion of minds." On doctrinal matters, he recommends and practices "great reserve."[11]

The cardinal rule is that the good guest does not usurp the place of the host. He does not take over the show. This is more than a matter of mere etiquette. In the last analysis, it is a question of relinquishing control, which, for historical reasons, is particularly difficult for us in the West. We tend, at times unconsciously, to dominate the discourse. We organize the meetings on our own ground and determine the rules, terms and procedures. To give up this position entails a risk. We may have to accept a different concept of dialogue altogether. As Panikkar says: "When I love, I go out, I give up, I am the guest."[12]

In addition to conventions, there are certain qualities, such as sincerity and good faith, that play a crucial part in human relations. We have to guard against the distortions that tend to arise from a desire to reduce the differences that make people uncomfortable. Unable to admit the real otherness of the other, some seek either to gloss over or to harmonize apparent contradictions. This inevitably leads to a reductionist version of their faith, and the superficial synthesis that emerges is what Hayek calls "une douce chimère," a pleasant pipe-dream.

There are even some who insist on treating differences as a "sign of unfinished work,"[14] to be relentlessly pursued by confrontation, with little concern for the disquiet, and even distress, involved in the quest for "coherence" (Cobb's chilling term). Happily, there are also those who hold that the aim of dialogue is not agreement but mutual understanding.[15]

One modern approach calls for the use of elaborate techniques, such as "bracketing" one's own beliefs, epoche—the suspension of personal convictions—and "passing over" temporarily into the other faith. The description of the personal practice of some individuals becomes a prescription for all those involved in the dialogue.

There are a number of reasons for eschewing artificial measures. People like to know where they are and what to expect of one another. They need to be able to count on the fact that others really mean what they say. If a situation is experienced as too confusing, particularly if participants sense an element of manipulation or duplicity, they will feel uneasy and even threatened. This creates a considerable barrier to the mutual trust that is vital for communication, and certainly for cooperation.

In fact, ordinary people accept differences quite naturally, especially those that are rooted in faith and identity. Merad appreciates that he has no access to the insights of the believer. The Tuareg understood that their Christian marabout could not fall in with their prayers,[16] still less suggest that they pray together, as might be recommended today. It is a necessary part of the dialogue to recognize that "there is also a limit to how far we can travel together."[17] To encourage unwarranted expectations is to set the stage for inevitable disillusion. Finally, techniques are undesirable if only because they demand a degree of concentration that distracts from the "patient and humble discipline of listening to others,"[18] which is the essence of any real conversation between real people.

We must remember, too, that real people have a history, a fact often disregarded in the present dialogue. From the time of the early conquests to the current bogey of "funda-mentalism," Christians have viewed Islam as a dangerous adversary. Muslims, in turn, have painful memories of the Crusades and the recent era of colonialism, and thy now face an invasion of Western secular and materialistic values.

It is sometimes suggested that we put all this behind us and start from a tabula rasa. But how can we shed bonds that are part of our identity as individuals and communities? It is sim-ply not possible to eliminate the past and start all over again. In reality, we come together with our history, which cannot be left at the door like a coat. We enter the dialogue fully clothed, and preferably in our usual dress rather than a peculiar garb donned for the occasion, rendering us barely recognizable to our own community and a mystery to others.

Those who recommend that we forgive and forget tend to assume that the words are inseparable. Yet it is possible to remember *and* forgive, and it may be the better way. To ignore the past is to ignore both its present consequences and the implications for the future. We need to take cognizance of our history in order to pave the way for the mutual forgive-ness of those who should be the "nearest in friendship."

As Merad insists, in relations between Muslims and authentic Christians, the most important word is friendship. Friendship, however, has to be about something. Although friends need not agree about the answer, they must agree that the question is one that matters to them both.[19] Partners in dialogue require themes that are mutually acceptable as the basis for discussion and common action. An example of such a theme is the one chosen by Merad, the imitation of Jesus.

To Christians, "following Jesus" is a familiar part of the original message, found in the teaching of Jesus and in the writings of Paul. From earliest times, the life and personal-ity of Jesus have been taken by his followers as a model for their response to God and to their fellow men.[20] Today many would echo Hick's affirmation: "We believe that he is so truly God's servant that in living as his disciples we are living according to the divine purpose."[21]

For Christians to favor the theme of imitation is to remain faithful to the Gospel story and to their personal commitment to Jesus. A Christian can speak from the center of the tradition that will be immediately recognized by other Christians—and, indeed, by Muslims—instead of relying on isolated texts, often with unusual, esoteric interpretations. In this way, genuine dialogue includes the witness to faith, what Buber call "speech from certainty to certainty,"[22] that distinguishes it from mere intellectual discussion.

For Muslims, a sincere veneration of Jesus is an integral part of their own faith. Merad states that Muslims regard Jesus with "an interest tinged with admiration," and that the Qur'an presents him as "a model of goodness, generosity, gentleness, filial devotion, and as an inexhaustible source of blessings and good things for men."[23] Muslims acknowledge Jesus' mission to teach and to act as a model. Imitation is what they would expect.

Thus Muslims can readily accept Jesus of Nazareth as a cornerstone of the dialogue, that is, Jesus without the theological interpretations of early and later Christianity. The idea of the divinity of Christ is an insurmountable obstacle and, as Ayoub graphically puts it, makes Muslims cringe.[24]

Of course a Christian will look at Jesus and discern something more. There is no call to renounce the traditional belief in the Incarnation, rather simply to do justice to that which both sides see and sanction. A Muslim can contemplate the life and teaching of the Nazarene, call to mind the Qur'anic allusions and, with Luke, hail a "prophet mighty in deed and word" (Luke 24:19). This surely provides more than Knitter's "shaky common ground" for a conversation.

A further advantage of the theme of imitation is its empha‐ sis on a way of life, an emphasis that can be fully endorsed by both sides. A true dialogue cannot be a purely academic exercise. There is a general sense that action is an integral part of the process. It has always been understood that faith must be reflected in the lives of the faithful. "By their fruits you shall know them" (Matthew 7:20) is a Christian princi‐ ple, and Jesus himself said: "Why call me 'Lord, Lord,' and do not the things which I say?" (Luke 6:46).

The Qur'an, too, repeatedly proclaims that true piety requires both belief and deeds of righteousness. Merad points out that, like Charles de Foucauld, Muslim saints strive to combine an active with a contemplative life. To promote humanitarian activities, far from resulting in a secular dia‐ logue, is a necessary course for both Christian and Muslim, and fitting response to the Qur'anic challenge to compete in good works (Q.2:148; 548).

In the past, the two sides have faced each another across the table and focused on the familiar fields of controversy. The battle lines have long been drawn, The contestants snipe at one another from fixed positions, and the operation ends in the inevitable stalemate. One way to break out of this pat‐ tern is to sit side by side facing the world and join together in the struggle against poverty, injustice and oppression.

It is not difficult to find shared concerns that make a natu‐ ral starting point for action. The common ground can evolve, instead of taking the form of preconditions. Working together and appreciating each other's distinctive contribution are both a means of communication and a unifying experience. While discussion tends to hold us apart, action can draw us together, and at times deeds are more eloquent than words.

What Knitter calls "action language" could also help us to dispense with a "dialoguespeak" that uses terms like under‐ standing and tolerance without reference to anything concrete at all. The theoretical debates of the veterans of dialogue often make them appear remote from the concerns of ordinary people who, it is hoped, will forge the friendships of the future.

On the matter of these concerns, there is one subject that cannot be avoided, and that is the subject of the Prophet. If Muslims willingly espouse the imitation of Jesus as a major theme for the dialogue, how can Christians respond, in the name of friendship? For the point about friendship is that it is reciprocal. To be a friend is to know and to care about what truly matters to the other. In this context, the issue that truly matters to Muslims more than anything else is the issue of the Prophet. It is the perennial "Muslim-to-Christian question":[25] What think ye of Muhammad?

The old response of antipathy and disparagement, sadly still far from uncommon, is seldom encountered in the dialogue. There the subject is most often met by silence—like the silence of Charles de Foucauld that drove Merad to wonder: "What were the Christian marabout's innermost feelings about Islam?"

We are confronted with the silence of the World Council of Churches, despite their ringing endorsements of dialogue.[26] We are faced, too, with the silence of the Vatican. For, although kind things are said about Islam in *Nostra Aetate* (1965), there is no mention of the Prophet—according to Küng, "out of embarrassment." The few who do speak his name tend to hedge their statements with qualifications: "in some sense a prophet,"[27] "an extraordinary [in contrast to an 'ordinary' or Christian] prophet."[28] This is cold comfort for Muslims.

Nasr maintains that "of the major elements of Islam the real significance of the Prophet is the least understood by non-Muslims."[29] Lack of understanding is the main reason for the bitter polemics over *The Satanic Verses* by Salman Rushdie. At the root of the affair lies the failure of non-Muslims to grasp the nature of the offense, and their inadequate and often hostile reaction to the Muslim outcry over the book.

It is hard to exaggerate the role of the Prophet in the Islamic world as a unifying force that transcends nation, culture and class. Iqbal truly wrote: "From Prophethood we all have the same melody."[30] The Prophet is "the touchstone of Islamic identity and loyalty,"[31] the focus of love and devotion, and the ideal model for Muslims. If his life is denigrated, so in turn are theirs. This accounts for the acute sense of personal injury reflected in the denunciations of Rushdie. Unless non-Muslims can come to respect and admire the Prophet, no real dialogue is possible, and there is certainly no hope of friendship.

If they aspire to be friends, Christians need to take some radical steps. More is required of the Church, ideally in the form of a binding statement—something, for example, in the spirit of Patriarch Timothy's acceptance that Muhammad "walked in the path of the prophets."[32] In the case of individuals and communities, knowledge of the Prophet's life and character (still rare, even in educated circles) is necessary, but not sufficient. Beyond that, we have to learn to honor his role in the religious consciousness of Muslims.

Definitions present theological problems that hark back to ancient disputes. The challenge here is to set definitions aside, and to respond generously and sympathetically to the millions who pattern their lives on the Prophet of Islam. Then, at last, we can say with Andrae: "I have looked into the face of a stranger and found a friend."[33]

The revelation of friendship is mirrored in Merad's deeply felt response to Charles de Foucauld and his imitation of Jesus. The Muslim scholar is able to see beyond the man, subject to the limitations of his time and place, to the true Christian whose gospel virtues are in harmony with the teaching of Islam.

Merad's work has a message of great consequence for the faltering Christian-Muslim dialogue, at a time when relations between Islam and the West are at a critical turning point. It underlines the need to move away from an academic practice that concentrates on divisive doctrinal issues, and to turn our mind to the concerns that bring us together. One of these is the concern expressed on both sides in discipleship.

We have seen how the imitation of Jesus has the power to evoke fellow feeling in a Muslim. The Christian guest in the House of Islam must not neglect the answering theme of the imitation of the Prophet (and how naturally Merad passes from one to the other!). There is an urgent need for deter-mined efforts on the part of non-Muslims. We must be will-ing to relinquish our position of dominance, and be prepared to listen and respond with the warm appreciation and the discretion that characterize the good guest.

This approach could help to widen the circle of partici-pants, as well as provide a natural meeting place for a gen-uine dialogue, so that we may talk to, not at and past, one another.[34] For as Ayoub, a masterly practitioner himself, declares: "True dialogue is conversation among persons and not a confrontation between ideas."[35]

Imitation, with its implicit ingredient of action, can foster the dialogue of words and deeds that is essential if Muslims and Christians are to become what they were meant to be, the "nearest in friendship." Only then can the age-old encounter take a new turning. The first step is for us in the West to learn how to be good guests. A large-hearted Muslim has shown the way, in a voice that needs not only to be heard, but to be answered. It is our move now, and the time is running out.

# Notes

## TRANSLATOR'S FOREWORD

1. A. Merad, *Charles de Foucauld au regard de l'Islam* (Paris, 1975). All the quotations are from my translation.

2. It is estimated that there are between 1.25 and 1.5 million Muslims in the United Kingdom, over 1.5 million Muslims in West Germany and over 3 million Muslims in France. See Jørgen S. Nielsen, *Muslims in Western Europe* (Edinburgh University Press, 1995).

3. See, for example, "An Islamic Perspective on Dialogue," articles translated by P. Johnstone in *Islamochristiana* 13 (1987), pp. 131–171. The point of view of a Christian is expressed by an American Jesuit in a personal communication: "If onetime I said that our dialogue is moribund, I can now confirm that. In fact, I'll go one step beyond. No signs of life since the feeble indications of last year [1993]. I am not sure I look forward to a re-incarnation. A resurrection is needed, involving a transformation, not merely a resuscitation."

4. The classic biography is R. Bazin, *Charles de Foucauld—Explorateur du Maroc—Ermite au Sahara* (Paris, 1921). Works available in English include: E. Hamilton, *The Desert My Dwelling Place, a Study of Charles de Foucauld* (London, 1968); A. Fremantle, *Desert Calling* (London, 1980); L. Sheppard, *Charles de Foucauld* (London, 1958); R. Voillaume, *Seeds of the Desert: The Legacy of Charles de Foucauld* (Herts, 1972).

5. Quoted by Peter France, *Hermits* (London, 1996), p. 134.

6. Voillaume, op. cit. p. 15.

7. Fremantle, op. cit. p. 239.

8. Sheppard, op. cit. p. 46.

9. Voillaume, op. cit. p. 80.

10. Bazin, op. cit. p. 204.

11. On the Tuareg, see J. Keenan, *The Tuareg: People of Ahaggar* (London, 1977); H. T. Norris, *The Tuaregs* (London, 1975).

12. The amenukal is the supreme elected chief of a Tuareg confederation.

13. Bazin, op. cit. p. 446.

14. France, op. cit. p. 155.

15. The Sanusiya was a genuine mystical order founded by the Grand Sanusi, one of the outstanding intellectuals of North Africa in the nineteenth century. French politicians tended to blame the brotherhood for any uprising or accident in the Sahara. The Sanusi would have been a natural scapegoat in a case like the killing of Foucauld. See B. G. Martin, *Muslim Brotherhoods in Nineteenth-Century Africa* (Cambridge University Press, 1976).

16. Charles de Foucauld had long been haunted by the idea of founding a new religious order and he framed a series of rules. His first rule for the Little Brothers of Jesus, drawn up in 1896 in Nazareth, was immediately vetoed by Abbé Huvelin, who wrote: "Your rule is completely impractical.... To tell the truth, it terrified me!... Do not, I beg of you, draft any rules!" (BAZ., p. 132). From 1899 to 1901, Foucauld produced a revised version and, finally, in 1902 and 1911, two further rules that reflected his mature thought. Abbé Huvelin was always troubled by the rigor of Foucauld's rules that prescribed a life of absolute poverty and extreme self-denial. At an early stage (in 1894), he remarked perceptively: "You are not at all suited to guide others" (BAZ., p. 127). In fact, the only man who, in 1906, attempted to share Foucauld's life, a sturdy Breton monk, collapsed and left after three months.

17. Hamilton, op. cit. p. 145.

18. T. S. Eliot, *Murder in the Cathedral*.

## CHAPTER I

1. In *Parole Donnée*, Paris, Julliard, 1962, p. 71.
2. Cf. A. Merad, *Ibn Bādīs, Commentateur du Coran*, Paris, P. Geuthner, 1971, p. 110.
3. In *Le Réformisme musulman en Algérie, de 1925 à 1940*, pp. 370–381.
4. For example, this prayer disseminated by the *Echo du Diocèse de Constantine et d'Hippone* (No. 3, Sunday, February 9, 1936): "Daily offering. I offer them up to you (prayers, deeds and afflictions of the day), in particular for the unity of Catholics and for the struggle against Islam"—"Missionary intention: struggle against Islam" (*Facsimile* in the Constantine reformist journal *al-Chihāb*, May 1936, p. 55).
5. Remarks reproduced in the journal *al-Chihāb* (January 1931, pp. 749–50), under the very significant title: "Christian missionary work is not propaganda with a temporal, colonialist end in view."
6. In a similar way, to console themselves for the rusticity of their life and the precariousness of their means of existence, simple folk in the Sahara used to say, speaking of Europeans: "They have the Earth, but we have the Heavens" (cf. the same idea in BAZ., p. 328). An identical feeling is expressed by Charles de Foucauld: "I am very, very, very happy: I have the Holy Sacrament, the love of Jesus.... Others have the earth, I have the good God..." (TEX.INED., p. 171).

## CHAPTER II

1. *Marabout* (orth., end of the sixteenth century: *morabuth*). Word of Arabic origin: *murābit*, soldier attached to the guard of a frontier post; then: religious dedicated to the defense of the borders of the Islamic empire; finally, any religious living in solitude (hermit). Distinguish *marabout* from *sharīf*: a person presumed to be descended from the Prophet and, as such, enjoying popular veneration. The term *sheikh*: master, refers to moral and intellectual authority (cf. the master at a Quranic school), and applies particularly to spiritual directors who may be marabouts and are also given the title *Sidi/Sidna* (My/Our Lord).

2. In this connection, it may be interesting to quote a biting
taunt by the great Algerian reformist writer Muhammad al-Bashīr
al-Ibrāhīmī (1889-1965): "It is clear that they (the marabouts) consider leaving a brotherhood—even for another one—a kind of
apostasy, for which the perpetrator will come, at his death, to a sad
end. The devil take them! To leave a brotherhood only means to
abandon one road to hell to return to the right way, or to leave one
road to hell only to fall into another!"

3. Note that South Oran was then under the influence of
Awlad Sidi Sheikh; the Tuareg were to some extent affected by the
sporadic impact on the central Sahara of the powerful Algerian-
Libyan brotherhood: the Sanusiya. Moreover, certain local
marabouts played a significant part in the moral and religious education of the Tuareg population. In particular must be mentioned:
Sid-Amer, and especially his son al-Bay, who exercised a definite
influence on the amenukal Moussa ag Amastane. The latter would
dedicate a pious phrase to these two personages in his long poetic
piece: "Men, Fear the Most High—who gave glory and veneration
to Sid-Amer—whose Son we visit in pilgrimage" [al-Bay]. (POES.
TOUAR., Vol. I, p. 392, v. 2-4).

Father de Foucauld was not unaware of the maraboutic influence on Tuareg society. However, it seems to us, he had a tendency
to see a marabout in anyone displaying religious zeal: "These
traders, he thinks, are almost all marabouts, men belonging to a
maraboutic tribe from Tidikelt, the Ahl Azzi; they will inevitably
bring with them a revival of Muslim fervor: all these men with
rosaries, praying and fasting in a conspicuous manner and loudly
proclaiming that they are marabouts to ensure a better reception,
will have a bad influence" (ECR.SPIR., p. 253).

4. Muslim religious institutions: headquarters (or outbuild-
ings) of religious orders, bringing together communities devoted
to a life of piety and study. As such, the zawāyā played an essential
part in the preservation and diffusion of Islamic culture in the
Maghrib, principally in the rural areas.

5. A soldier from the garrison at Béni-Abbès had been placed
at Charles de Foucauld's disposal to help him in his hermitage.

6. To have some idea of the solicitude of Charles de Foucauld, "country doctor," one has only to glance at the meticulous lists of medicaments he prepared in anticipation of his rounds through the oases and the Hoggar (see: LES., pp. 262–264).

7. It is interesting to compare this Quranic concept of piety, that exalts the values of suffering and sacrifice, with these reflections taken from a letter from Charles de Foucauld to his family: "It would have been quite easy for God to create a world where there would be no place for evil; yet he did not wish to.... Why? No doubt because 'to conquer without danger is to triumph without glory.' Take away evil, and you take away suffering, sacrifice, martyrdom, courage, devotion, heroism and charity, all virtues that only develop in the face of misfortune or danger" (TEX. INED., p. 153).

8. This term is part of the Quranic vocabulary. From the basic meaning of "guide" (he who offers himself as a guide, or is accepted as such), it has taken on several meanings in usage:

(a) *Cultural sense:* the person appointed by the community (and increasingly, in contemporary Muslim societies, by the authorities), to lead the congregational prayer—at the mosque—and to deliver the Friday sermon.

(b) *Political sense:* the head of the community (local or national); taken in the absolute sense, this term designates the supreme head of the universal Islamic community (synonym: *caliph*). The office of the supreme *imāmat* is, as we know, vacant at present in the Muslim world (since 1924).

(c) *Cultural sense:* any doctor of religious knowledge accepted as an authority throughout the Muslim world (like the former grand *muftī* of Egypt, Muhammad Abduh (1849–1905).

## CHAPTER III

1. In this connection, see the testimony of Major Robert Hérisson (a Protestant), describing a scene he witnessed around 1909–1910, in the course of which Charles de Foucauld acted as arbitrator for the Tuareg in the case of a camel theft, in: BAZ., p. 381.

2. On the notion of the "Call to Good" in Islam and the doctrinal principles that make it a major obligation in Islamic ethics,

see, among others: Léon Bercher, "De l'obligation d'ordonner le Bien et d'interdire le Mal selon al-Ghazālī," in: I.B.L.A. (Tunis), 1st and 3rd quarter 1955; Louis Gardet, *Dieu et la Destinée de l'Homme*, Paris, J. Vrin, 1967, pp. 445ff.

3. Although Charles de Foucauld was kind to the Tuareg and constantly at their disposal, one wonders if he really did have a high regard for them, when his vision of Saharan Muslim society was so tainted by profound pessimism. Witness these disen-chanted reflections (extracts from a letter to his brother-in-law, Raymond de Blic, on December 9, 1907): "If there is so much evil in Christian countries, think what it must be like in countries where there is, as it were, only evil, where good is almost entirely absent: There is nothing but lying, deceit, guile, every kind of envy, violence, and what ignorance and barbarity! The grace of God can do anything, but in the face of such moral wretched-ness...it is clear that human means are powerless and that God alone can bring about such a great transformation" (BAZ., p. 350).

4. "Do his fine qualities exclude ambition, sensuality and, deep in his heart, contempt and hatred for non-Muslims? I do not think so..." (BAZ., p. 322).

5. In a letter to Mgr. Livinhac (October 26, 1905), he describes him in these terms: "He is extremely intelligent, filled with good intentions, and concerned exclusively with the good of Muslims and the Tuareg. A large-minded person, he devotes his life to pro-moting peace among the Tuareg and protecting the weak from the violence of the strong, gaining thereby, as well as for his generos-ity, piety, good nature and courage, universal veneration from In-Salah to Timbuktu; the good that he does and his efforts for peace and justice are not restricted to the Hoggar (...); his moder-ation, his desire for peace and his constant support of the poor and oppressed against injustice are remarkable" (BAZ., p. 321). A little later in the same letter, he emphasizes "his justice, his courage, and the nobility and generosity of his character" (p. 322).

This moral portrait should be compared to Charles de Foucauld's biographical note on Moussa ag Amastane the poet, in POES. TOUAR., Vol. I, pp. 366–368. This note retraces the whole political career of the amenukal of the Hoggar, up to the date of his submission to the French (1904). It says, in conclusion: "France owes him a debt for having found, when it occupied Ahaggar, not a desert, without fields, flocks, or inhabitants, but a country with arable land, cattle and an intelligent, open-minded and obedient population (Ibid., p. 368).

6. "Moussa is wonderful" (GOR., p. 313).—"Moussa has been very good since the beginning of the war" (GOR., p. 305).— "Moussa has proved his loyalty so clearly and steadfastly that the loyalty of all his subjects has been confirmed" (GOR., p. 306).

7. See the details on this subject furnished by Charles de Foucauld in a letter to Père Guérin, July 22, 1907, in BAZ., pp. 349–350.

8. Moussa ag Amastane (born around 1867) was no longer a young man in need of the enlightened advice of a mentor. At the time of his submission to the French, at the beginning of 1904, he was nearly thirty-seven years of age. Charles de Foucauld (born in 1858) met him a few months later, on June 25, 1904.

9. Charles de Foucauld was aware of this ambiguity and asked the same question about Muslims: "Will they know how to distin-guish between soldiers and priests, to see us as servants of God, envoys of peace and charity, universal brothers? I do not know..." (ECR.SPIR., p. 252).

10. See details of his advice in: BAZ., pp. 323–325, from a pri-vate diary of Charles de Foucauld, that records on several pages: "Things to say to Moussa" and "Letters written to Moussa."

11. The oral literature of the Tuareg, a good part of which was collected by Charles de Foucauld, provides ample information about the Tuareg population's reaction to the French presence. Some satires label as apostates those Tuareg who had accepted submission to the French or come to terms with them. See, for example: POES. TOUAR., Vol. I, p. 251, v. 1; p. 253, v. 3; p. 466, v. 1: "I left Amgha—which has apostatized..." Cf. Charles de Foucauld's explanatory note: "The Author says that the valley of Amgha has apostatized, because of the presence in that valley of Major Laperrine and his detachment."

12. Infidels, pagans, and barbarians are terms often employed by Charles de Foucauld for the Muslim peoples of Morocco,

Algeria and the Sahara. Cf. ECR.SPIR, p. 253: "Thank God, Hoggar and Taïtok are scarcely Muslim except in name..." It is fair to note that, at the same time, Tuareg hostile to the French presence had no hesitation in calling Christians "pagans" and infidels. Cf. POES.TOUAR., Vol. I, p. 285, v. 3; p. 495, v. 1–2; p. 497, v. 2–3. In reference to the battle of Tit (1909): "On the Day of the pagans (i.e., the French), there was an afternoon when we used gunpowder and the bullets danced the dance of the blacks."

13. A systematic study of *Poésies Touarègues—Dialecte de l'Ahaggar,* collected by Fr. de Foucauld and published by André Basset (Paris, Vol. I, 1925; Vol. II, 1930), would demonstrate the extent to which Islam pervades Tuareg life.

14. Cf. similarly: ECR.SPIR., pp. 237, 238, 250, 257, 263; *Dir.,* p. 101; etc.

15. The act of faith is called in Arabic *aqd:* knot, knotting. To believe is not only to adhere, it is to knot in one's being something one regards as essential. This act is all the stronger because it assumes simple beliefs (faith in the oneness of God; faith in the mission of Muhammad), absolutized by community tradition, and able, by this very fact, to engender total commitment.

16. To his cousin, Madame de Bondy (May 11, 1909): "I want to ask you for twenty or so ordinary rosaries, made of wood, but solidly mounted in iron or copper...—They are for the Muslims, whom I am teaching to pray saying on the little beads: 'My God, I love you with all my heart'" (GOR., p. 240). On June 29, 1909, he submitted to Mgr. Guérin "his plan for a Charity-Rosary intended for infidels" (GOR.,p. 242).

17. Charles de Foucauld was conscious of the reserve, if not distrust, that he inspired in some Tuareg: "What have I come to do?" he writes, interpreting their feelings (cf. OEUV.SPIR., p. 640).

## CHAPTER IV

1. A European's impressions of the space and light of the Great South are admirably described by the painter and writer Eugène Fromentin (1820–1876) in his book *Un Eté dans le Sahara* (ed. Plon). See for example pp. 174–176. Cf. also the personal

impressions of Carlo Carretto in his *Lettres du Désert* (Apostolat des Editions, 1973).

2. Extract from a Lecture by General Niéger, published in the journal *Construire* (Paris), Vol. XIII, 1943, pp. 185–186.

3. E./F. Gautier, "Deux Algériens" [the biologist Emile Maupas and Father de Foucauld], in *La Revue de Paris*, September–October 1919, pp. 285–315.

4. *Ibid.*, p. 290.

5. *Ibid.*, p 291.

6. *Ibid.*, p. 291.

7. *Ibid.*, p. 291.

8. *Ibid.*, p. 291.

9. Gobineau, *Nouvelles Asiatiques*, Classiques Garnier, Paris, p. 320.

10. One must remember that after the opening of the Suez Canal (1869), and especially after the British occupation of Egypt (1882), Near Eastern Islam began to lose its mystery in European intellectual and political circles.

11. A remarkable example of this awareness is provided by the conclusions of the senatorial commission of inquiry sent to Algeria in 1891 (see in particular the evidence of Jules Ferry, president of this commission, Ferdinand Buisson, Maurice Wahl and Franck Chauveau). Cf. Sénat, *Commission d'Etude des Questions Algériennes. Dépositions du 1er mai au 20 juillet 1891*, Paris, 1891.

12. 3rd ed., revised and expanded, Paris, Lévy, 1866, 8ᵉ, 486 p.

13. The text of this Lecture appears in *Les Oeuvres Complètes d'Ernest Renan*, definitive edition by Henriette Psichari, Paris, Calmann-Lévy, 1947, Volume I, pp. 944–960.

14. Take the example of Guy de Maupassant (1850–1893). In the course of his travels in Algeria (1881) and Tunisia (1888–1889), "that fanatical land," the great writer seems to have tried to record mainly whatever would depict "the fatalistic spirit of the Oriental" (cf. *Au Soleil*, 1884; *Sur l'Eau*, 1888; *La Vie Errante*, 1890).

15. *L'Armée et la Mission de la France en Afrique*, by Mgr. The Archbishop of Algiers [Charles Martial Allemand-Lavigerie], Speech given on April 25, 1875 in Algiers Cathedral, Algiers, A. Jourdan, 64 p. (p. 5).

16. Some examples: p. 9, "barbaric regions" (the lands of North Africa); p. 11: "barbarity" of the Turks, "supported by the barbaric population of Africa"; p. 14: "these barbarians (the Dey of Algiers and his auxiliaries); p. 17 "the barbarian troops" (of Algiers); p. 31, the Emir Abdel Kader is described as a "scholar and poet insofar as a barbarian can be"; p. 34, there is reference to his "barbarian instinct"; p. 60: Algeria is called "a barbaric realm"; etc.

17. And even when it concerns the present situation of "all these people, today lost in death" (*L'Armée et la Mission de la France en Afrique*, p. 64).

18. *Ibid.*, p. 24.

19. *Recueil de Lettres* published by Mgr. The Archbishop of Algiers on *Les Oeuvres et Missions Africaines*, Paris, Plon, 1869, p. 41.

20. *Ibid.*, p. 41.

21. *Ibid.*, p. 10.

22. *Ibid.*, p. 10.

23. Racine, *Bérénice*, Act I, Scene IV.

24. Card. Lavigerie, *L'Armée et la Mission de la France en Afrique*, p. 6.

25. This is the theme developed by Card. Lavigerie in his discourse on April 25, 1875 in Algiers Cathedral. To quote some significant extracts: "(...)In the same way, to revive the famous land of Tertullian, Cyprian, Augustine, and so many great men, he [God] chose an army, the army of France.

"Do not be surprised at the choices of Providence. Together with the apostles of truth, men of war are those whom God involves most visibly in his action in the world. To the first, he entrusts the designs of his mercy, to the second, the decrees of his justice.

"When a nation takes up arms to serve the great causes of humanity and justice, when this nation bears the light and name of Jesus Christ all the way to the barbaric regions, and, with a high sense of duty, is committed to the sacrifice of wealth and blood in order to wrest a people from death...one must proclaim, in so generous an enterprise, an action superior to man's, and confess, with the Prophet (Ezekiel), that it is God Himself who inspires this selfless courage....

"From this description, who will not recognize the history of our African conquest, and if ever France received a mission from above, when was it more evident?" (*L'Armée et la Mission de la France en Afrique*, pp. 5–7).

## CHAPTER V

1. He was formerly second lieutenant with him in the Chasseurs d'Afrique.

2. Between 1902 and 1904, three of the six large Tuareg fractions submitted to Major Laperrine: the Taïtok (Ahnet): mid-1902; the Iforas (East Adrar): November 1903; the Hoggar (Jebel Ahaggar): January 1904. This last fraction was the most important and warlike of all.

3. The same opinion, expressed by him in almost identical terms, on September 21, 1912: "If France does not administer the natives in her colony better than she has done, she will lose it..." (ECR.SPIR., p. 243).

4. Especially the slaves. Fr. de Foucauld led a veritable campaign against slavery ("this huge and monstrous injustice"), in the Saharan oases and among the Tuareg. Cf. OEUV.SPIR., "Sur l'Esclavage," pp. 616–626.

5. These were the "Young Algerians," who gave rise to much talk at the beginning of this century. On the ideas and aspirations of this French-educated Muslim élite, see Philippe Millet, "Les Jeunes Algériens," in *La Revue de Paris*, November–December 1913, pp. 158–180.

6. On the colonial forces of opposition to plans to extend French education to Algerian Muslims, see our study: "Regards sur l'Enseignment des Musulmans en Algérie (1880–1960)," in *Confluent*, Paris, No. 32–33. June–July 1963, pp. 596–645.

7. In this matter, Charles de Foucauld labored under the curious delusion that education would be enough to turn Muslims away from their faith: "For Islam," he asserted, "cannot hold out in the face of education; history and philosophy refute it conclusively: it falls like night before day" (ECR.SPIR., p. 256).

8. "I have two hermitages, 1500 kilometers apart. I spend three months in one in the North, six months in the one in the South, three months coming and going every year" (ECR.SPIR., p. 258).

9. Fr. de Foucauld kept himself regularly up to date with events on the Algerian/Tripolitanian border (1915-1916), so that he could immediately inform General Laperrine. "In two years, he sent forty/one letters to his friend to give him information on events in the Sahara" (GOR., p. 298).

10. On the man of God's attitude to the world of politics, Charles de Foucauld gives us these precious words to meditate on: "We must not interfere in the secular government, no one is more convinced of this than I am, but we must 'love justice and hate iniquity,' and when the secular government commits a great injus/tice against those who are to some degree in our charge (...), we must speak out, for we are the ones who represent justice and truth on this earth, and we do not have the right to be 'sleeping sentinels,' 'silent dogs,' 'uncaring shepherds' (OEUV.SPIR., p. 617).

11. Cf. a similar opinion expressed by Captain Dinaux, chief of the annexe at In/Salah, in a report to the Governor General. "The Father's reputation for holiness, and the results that he has already achieved healing the sick, will do more to extend our influ/ence and win people over to our ideas than a permanent occupa/tion of the country..." (LES., p. 132).

12. It is not our intention, given the limitations of this little book, to go into the circumstances of Father Charles de Foucauld's death. The thesis, too often repeated, that the Father's assassination was perpetrated by agents of the Sanusiya—ex officio—appears to us to be without any foundation. It is true that this powerful Algerian/Libyan brotherhood played a not insignificant role in the Saharan population's resistance to the French encroachment. This was a political choice (with religious motivations, admittedly) in the course of which supporters of the Sanusiya had carried out a relentless struggle against the French forces. But as a religious movement, the Sanusi brotherhood saw it as their duty to respect Christians, as con/firmed by the directives and constant practice of its Grand Master. (In this connection see the account given by a highly placed Tunisian,

Si Mohammed Ben Othmane El-Hachaichi, on his return from a period of study at Kufra, the seat of the said brotherhood: "Chez les Senoussis et les Touaregs," *Revue de Paris,* August 15, 1901, pp. 677-709). It would therefore be unfair to blame this religious brotherhood for a crime that horrifies every Muslim.

The truth demands that events be viewed more simply. Since the beginning of the war (autumn 1914), insecurity was rife in northern Algeria as it was in the territories of the south. Poorly guarded prisons and penitentiaries were emptied. Bands of criminals formed almost everywhere, sowing terror in the countryside. Hamlets were abandoned, with their crops. The new, more serious outbreak of crime is officially established. (Cf. the speech of Governor General Lutaud to the *Financial Delegations,* on June 7, 1915, in *Renseignements Coloniaux,* supplement to *L'Afrique Française,* No. 6-7, June-July 1915, pp. 105-112, with the title "L'Algérie pendant la Guerre" (see p. 109, col. B, p. 3). Moreover, Algerian Muslims (landowners, traders and travelers) were to suffer from this insecurity more than the French *(ibid.).* In the Saharan zone, rezzous (bands of looters) attacked encampments, cattle farms and grain caravans.

The episode at Tamanrasset (December 1, 1916) was part of this long series of exactions and crimes. Informed (?) of the store of arms that Charles de Foucauld had finally accepted for the defense of his hermitage-fortress (the construction of which was finished in October 1916), and no doubt tempted by the hope of finding money and substantial provisions (the Father received up to three camel-loads of supplies), the looters probably expected to carry out a doubly advantageous operation without striking a blow. It is worth recalling that in his official report (Sept. 11, 1917), Captain Depommier did not overlook the possible attraction of the stock of arms and munitions consigned to Father de Foucauld: this led him to pose the question: "Would he have been assassinated if he had had no arms with him?" (BAZ., p. 459, 1st p.).

Under the circumstances, it is only right to reduce this affair to the dimensions of one of a number of tragic episodes that took place daily in Algeria in this unsettled time of war. (See the many events reported by Jean Melia in *L'Algérie et la Guerre* (1914-1918, p. 250).

An innocent victim—among so many others—this is how Charles de
Foucauld appears to us on the day of his death, which was the reflection of a whole life of sacrifice: an unjust, violent death, that he had
accepted in advance, as if it were the natural fulfillment of his destiny. Moreover, in one form or another, the risk of an accident had
continually threatened the great hermit's existence, in a region
where the ordinarily harsh and dangerous life had been considerably
aggravated by repercussions of the international conflict which in the
end swept the Sahara into its maelstrom.

13. This quotation recalls a saying of the Prophet, calling to
witness the crowd of Believers, at a time of his last pilgrimage to
Mecca (March 632). Aware of his approaching end, Muhammad
addressed his final exhortations to the Community in a *Farewell
Sermon* in which the main passages were punctuated by the question: "Have I accomplished my mission?" And each time, the
crowed replied: "By God, yes!" The broad outline of this *Farewell
Sermon* can be found in M. Gaudefroy-Demombynes, *Mahomet*,
Paris, Albin Michel, 1957, p. 219.


## TRANSLATOR'S AFTERWORD

MERAD'S RESPONSE TO CHARLES DE FOUCAULD

1. M. Praz, *The Romantic Agony* (Oxford, 1951), p. 275.
2. R. Bazin, *Charles de Foucauld—Explorateur du Maroc—
Ermite au Sahara* (Paris, 1921), pp. 422-23.
3. *Ibid.* p. 449.
4. *Ibid.* p. 443.
5. C.R. Ageron, *Politiques Coloniales au Magreb* (Paris,
1973), p. 120.
6. E. Said, *Orientalism* (London, 1978), p. 204.
7. Bazin, op. cit. p. 401.
8. *Ibid.* p. 444.
9. W. Wordsworth, *Tintern Abbey*.
10. Said, op. cit. p. 228.
11. On this point, see A. Charfi, "Christianity in the Qur'an
Commentary of Tabarī," *Islamochristiana* 6 (1980), pp. 105-148.

12. This passage should not be invoked indiscriminately. As McAuliffe shows, Qur'anic commentators through the ages have understood it to refer to a limited number of Christians. For example, al-Razi (d. 1150) cautions that "certainly the verse does not mean all Christians...given the visible evidence of their animosity toward Muslims." J. McAuliffe, *Qur'anic Christians* (New York, 1991), p. 210. See also M. Borrmans, "Le Commentaire du Manār à propos du verset coranique sur l'amitié des musulmans pour les chrétiens (5, 82), *Islamochristiana* 1 (1975), pp. 71-86.

13. See G. Anawati, "'Īsā." In *The Encyclopedia of Islam*, 4, pp. 81-86. New edition. Leiden, 1954; M. Hayek, *Le Christ de l'Islam* (Paris, 1959); K. Cragg, *Jesus and the Muslim* (London, 1985); G. Parrinder, *Jesus in the Qur'an* (London, 1976).

14. Quoted in M. Smith, *Studies in Early Mysticism in the Near and Middle East* (London, 1931), pp. 117-18.

15. *Ibid.* pp. 92-93.

16. See T. Andrae, *In the Garden of Myrtles* (Albany, 1987), "Islam and Christianity," pp. 7-32.

17. V. Crapanzano, *The Hamadsha* (Berkeley, 1973), p. 1. On maraboutism, see also E. Gellner, *Saints of the Atlas* (London, 1969); J. S. Trimingham, *The Sufi Orders in Islam* (Oxford, 1971); R. Montagne, *The Berbers, Their Social and Political Organization* (London, 1973).

18. Marabout comes from the Arabic al-murābit, an ascetic living in a ribāt or frontier fort. The root meaning of the word is to bind, tie or attach (Wehr's *Dictionary of Modern Written Arabic*). Geertz describes a marabout as a man "shackled to God." C. Geertz, *Islam Observed* (London, 1968), p. 43.

19. Andrae, op. cit. p. 3.

20. J. Keenan, *The Tuareg: People of Ahaggar* (London, 1977), p. 154.

21. Gellner, op. cit. p. 146.

22. T. S. Eliot, *The Family Reunion*.

SOME LESSONS FOR THE CHRISTIAN-MUSLIM DIALOGUE

1. R. Panikkar, *The Intrareligious Dialogue* (New York, 1978), pp. 26-37.

2. A concept developed by G. R. Dunstan, *The Artifice of Ethics* (London, 1974), pp. 1-17. See also D. Emmet, *Rules, Roles and Relations* (London, 1966).

3. Quoted by H. Mason in *Memoir of a Friend: Louis Massignon* (Indiana, 1988), p. 89.

4. L. Swidler in L. Swidler, J. Cobb, P. Knitter, M. Hellwig, *Death or Dialogue?* (London, 1990), p. 61.

5. P. Knitter in *Death or Dialogue?* p. 126.

6. This is stated as an axiom by P. Knitter in *No Other Name?* (London, 1985), pp. 211 ff.

7. P. Knitter in *Death or Dialogue?* p. 31.

8. Jerome Hall Dialogue at Harvard Divinity School, October 16, 1984. My own notes.

9. This is a familiar suggestion. For example, Räisänen claims that "a really penetrating dialogue between the two faiths can only begin when both sides are prepared to take historical criticism seriously." H. Räisänen, "The Portrait of Jesus in the Qur'an: Reflections of a Biblical Scholar," *The Muslim World*, LXX (April 1980), pp. 122-33.

10. Re this sura, McAuliffe writes: "Avoidance, physical and verbal restraint, courteous rejoinder, and simply taking one's leave of an antagonist are all mentioned by the commentators as suitable responses to the overtures of hostile or ignorant nonbe-lievers." Op. cit., p. 259.

11. A common practice among Islamic theologians, according to S. Balić, "The Image of Jesus in Contemporary Islamic Theology," in A. Schimmel and A. Falaturi (eds.), *We Believe in One God* (London, 1979), p. 3.

12. R. Panikkar, "The Unknown Christ of Hinduism," in J. Hick and P. Hebblethwaite (eds.), *Christianity and Other Religions* (Philadelphia, 1980), p. 146.

13. M. Hayek, op. cit. p. 9.

14. J. Cobb in *Death or Dialogue?* p. 121.

15. A fine example is R. M. Speight's *Christian-Muslim Relations* (Hartford, 1983).

16. The Tuareg teacher who worked with Foucauld said: "We know quite well that the marabout could not tell us to pronounce the Shahada. There is no doubt about it. It would be incompatible

with his position as a Catholic priest. We all know it." Quoted in R. Bazin, op. cit. p. 406.

17. M. Ayoub, "Divine Revelation and the Person of Jesus Christ," a lecture presented at the Muslim/Christian Colloquium (Toronto, 1989).

18. Roger Hooker, quoted in K. Cracknell, *Towards a New Relationship* (London, 1986) p. 144.

19. C. S. Lewis, "Friendship," in *The Four Loves* (London, 1963), pp. 55–84.

20. For the importance of this theme in early Christianity, see G. N. Stanton, *Jesus of Nazareth in New Testament Preaching* (London, 1974).

21. J. Hick in *Christianity and Other Religions*, op cit. p. 186.

22. M. Buber, *Between Man and Man* (London, 1961), p. 24.

23. A. Merad, "Christ According to the Qur'an," *Encounter*, No. 69 (November 1980).

24. M. Ayoub, Toronto lecture, op cit.

25. K. Cragg, *Muhammad and the Christian* (London, 1984), p. 3.

26. *Guidlines on Dialogue with People of Living Faiths and Ideologies*, World Council of Churches (1979).

27. W. M. Watt, *Muslim/Christian Encounters* (London, 1991), p. 148

28. H. Küng, op cit.

29. S. H. Nasr, *Ideals and Realities of Islam* (London, 1979), p. 69.

30. Quoted in A. Schimmel, *And Muhammad is His Messenger* (Chapel Hill, 1985), p. 252.

31. K. Cragg, *Muhammad and the Christian*, p. 71.

32. Cited by David Kerr in his timely chapter "The Prophet Mohammad in Christian Theological Perspective," in *Islam in a World of Diverse Faiths*, edited by D. Cohn/Sherbok (London, 1991), p. 129.

33. T. Andrae, op cit. p. 5.

34. Cf. M. Buber, op cit. p. 64.

35. M. Ayoub, "Muslim Views of Christianity: Some Modern Examples," *Islamochristiana* 10 (1984), pp. 49–70.